African American History

An Enthralling Overview of Major Events and Figures in Black History

© Copyright 2025 - All rights reserved.

The content contained within this book may not be reproduced, duplicated, or transmitted without direct written permission from the author or the publisher.

Under no circumstances will any blame or legal responsibility be held against the publisher, or author, for any damages, reparation, or monetary loss due to the information contained within this book, either directly or indirectly.

Legal Notice:

This book is copyright protected. It is only for personal use. You cannot amend, distribute, sell, use, quote, or paraphrase any part, or the content within this book, without the consent of the author or publisher.

Disclaimer Notice:

Please note the information contained within this document is for educational and entertainment purposes only. All effort has been executed to present accurate, up-to-date, reliable, and complete information. No warranties of any kind are declared or implied. Readers acknowledge that the author is not engaging in the rendering of legal, financial, medical, or professional advice. The content within this book has been derived from various sources. Please consult a licensed professional before attempting any techniques outlined in this book.

By reading this document, the reader agrees that under no circumstances is the author responsible for any losses, direct or indirect, that are incurred as a result of the use of the information contained within this document, including, but not limited to, errors, omissions, or inaccuracies.

Free limited time bonus

Stop for a moment. We have a free bonus set up for you. The problem is this: we forget 90% of everything that we read after 7 days. Crazy fact, right? Here's the solution: we've created a printable, 1-page pdf summary for this book that you're reading now. All you have to do to get your free pdf summary is to go to the following website:
https://livetolearn.lpages.co/enthrallinghistory/

Or, Scan the QR code!

Once you do, it will be intuitive. Enjoy, and thank you!

Table of Contents

INTRODUCTION 1
CHAPTER 1: FROM SLAVERY TO EMANCIPATION........................4
CHAPTER 2: THE STRUGGLE FOR CIVIL RIGHTS POST CIVIL-WAR 18
CHAPTER 3: THE HARLEM RENAISSANCE 27
CHAPTER 4: THE CIVIL RIGHTS MOVEMENT: HEROES, TRIUMPHS AND PROTESTS..32
CHAPTER 5: THE QUEST FOR RACIAL EQUALITY IN THE 1960S AND 1970S 39
CHAPTER 6: THE RISE OF THE BLACK ENTREPRENEUR 52
CHAPTER 7: WOMEN WHO SHAPED HISTORY 60
CHAPTER 8: THE EVOLUTION OF BLACK MUSIC 72
CHAPTER 9: VOTING RIGHTS AND BLACK LIVES MATTER 84
CHAPTER 10: A COLORED LEGACY: REFLECTIONS AND HOPE FOR THE FUTURE 90
CONCLUSION 95
HERE'S ANOTHER BOOK BY ENTHRALLING HISTORY THAT YOU MIGHT LIKE..97
FREE LIMITED TIME BONUS...98
BIBLIOGRAPHY AND FURTHER READING 99
IMAGE SOURCES 102

Introduction

African American history can be terrible to read about, but it is also incredibly inspiring. It's dreadful because of the sheer inhumanity with which African Americans have been treated over the centuries, but the massive achievements of African Americans, individually and as a people, are an inspiration. Time and time again, progress has been clawed back, and the struggle for equality and respect has had to start all over again. Yet, in 200 years, we've gone from African Americans being slaves to an African American president.

And we *should* read about it. It's a huge part of the history of the United States, and an important one. African American history isn't just for African Americans. John Hope Franklin, one of the founders of Black history as a discipline, claimed that Black history involved rewriting the history of America itself. If we don't understand the Black contribution to today's America, how can we understand the whole picture? Understanding this history can help us understand why African Americans sometimes have a very different perspective on things than White Americans and Americans from other ethnicities.

The African American contribution to American achievement has often been overlooked, making Black people "invisible" in much of American history. Here are a few big contributions that tend to go unnoticed:

- York, a scout and trapper, played an important role in ensuring the success of the Lewis and Clark Expedition. He was a slave, although on the expedition he had a vote in all decisions and was allowed a gun. He helped feed the expedition's members through his hunting and fascinated the Native Americans they met en route, making relations with the tribes easier for the White members of the expedition. He was the first African American to reach the Pacific. However, after the expedition, he was not given any monetary bonus or land, and Clark refused to emancipate him.

- The slave Onesimus introduced the concept of inoculation against smallpox to Cotton Mather. Inoculation was already practiced in Africa, but many White Americans were skeptical. Cotton Mather generally got the credit, until very recently.
- African American cowboys like Bose Ikard, Nat Love, Jesse Stahl, Mary Fields (the first star route postwoman) and Isam Dart contributed to the development of the western frontier. A third of all settlers in the West were African American and Hispanic.

Isam (or Isom) Dart. [1]

- Matthew Henson accompanied Robert Peary on his expeditions to the Arctic. Though he published his account of the expeditions in 1912, he was not made a member of the Explorers Club until 1937. (It would be gratifying to say he was the first man to reach the North Pole, but later analysis of Peary's records suggests the expedition terminated some sixty miles or so short of the pole itself.)

This book will explain African American history from the beginnings of African involvement in the Americas to the present day. You won't need any existing knowledge. Everything you need to get a grasp of the basic facts and ideas is included in this book, as well as suggestions for further reading. It's a comprehensive history that will give you a good understanding of major political and cultural movements and the latest views on questions such as reparations for slavery.

You'll also learn about fascinating individuals like Josephine Baker—a singer turned French Resistance heroine—Absalom F. Boston, who captained his own whaling ship with an all-Black crew, and heroes of the civil rights movement like Martin Luther King Jr. and Rosa Parks.

Chapter 1: From Slavery to Emancipation

Slavery casts a huge shadow over the history of the Americas, and its impact is still felt today.

Some commentators believed Jesse Jackson's 1988 campaign for the Democratic presidential ticket was too focused on the issue of slavery. But, in fact, you can rarely get away from it when you're talking about the history of African Americans.

Slavery existed long before the United States became independent. It started with Portuguese and Spanish explorers, who from the fifteenth century onward used slavery to help them colonize the Americas. They brought slaves from Africa, buying them from African rulers who had generally enslaved them as prisoners of war.

Not all the early colonies had slavery. In Northern colonies, there were many free Black people in the early years of colonization by the British, but gradually, slavery became acceptable in most of the North.

The triangular trade developed in the seventeenth and eighteenth centuries. Slave ships exported European goods to Africa in return for slaves; the slaves were taken to the New World via the Middle Passage and sold there; cash crops such as cotton, sugar and tobacco were then exported to Europe as payment for the slaves.

Slavery was particularly important in the Southern colonies and (later) states, where it became a major part of the economy due to the use of the plantation system. Slaves provided the labor for huge estates with highly concentrated ownership rather than the more fragmented style of agriculture in the North, based around family farms. This would lead to tensions within the United States—between free states and slave states, North and South—which eventually exploded in the Civil War.

Initially, most slaves came to North America indirectly via the Caribbean, where plantations already relied heavily on the institution of slavery. In some ways, it was like indentured service. Many White people were indentured, not actually enslaved, since they owed several years of service to a master in return for a debt—usually their fare to the New World. In the early seventeenth century, some Black slaves were set free and assigned land for their use when they had served a certain amount of time, in the same way as White indentured servants.

There were also free Black men, such as Anthony Johnson, who had arrived in Virginia as "Antonio" (clearly from a Spanish-speaking colony) in 1621. He gained his freedom and became a major landowner who called his estate "Angola" (his homeland). He also owned slaves himself, and in 1655 sued a White neighbor for the return of a runaway. However, by the 1650s racial distinctions had hardened, and in the 1670 slave status became hereditary.

Slavery took a huge human toll. Slaves were always chained onboard ship; if they were not prevented, many tried to leap into the sea to drown rather than be carried away. In 1807, Africans who had arrived by boat in Charleston starved themselves to death rather than live as slaves.[i] Suicides were frequent among African Americans. Some slave mothers even killed their children to save them from slavery.

The journey from Africa to the New World took three months. Slave ships were overcrowded, which enabled disease to take hold. Smallpox and "the flux" (diarrhea or dysentery) killed many slaves en route. Twelve million slaves were shipped to the New World, but a third of the slaves may have died before shipping, and nearly two million died before reaching America. Many were never able to recover from the ordeal of the passage. A quarter of newly arrived slaves in Virginia died within a year of arrival.

---

[i] J.H. Franklin and E.B. Higginbotham, *From Slavery to Freedom: A History of African Americans* (McGraw Hill, 2011), 153.

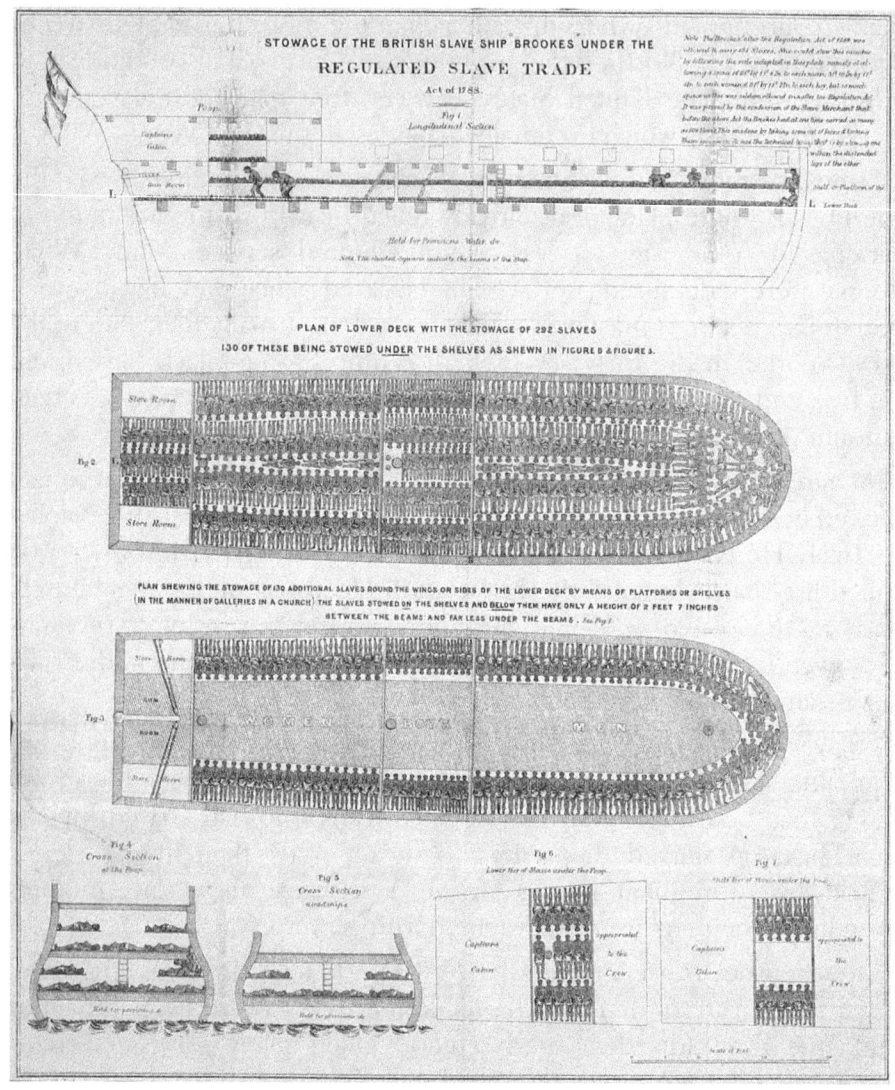

Plan of the slave ship Brookes.[2]

The human cost also includes the children and grandchildren of those slaves, who were born as slaves in the New World, as well as the continued prejudice and economic disadvantage for Black people in the United States.

Slaves had no rights at all, not even the right to family life. Families were often split up on an owner's death, when the estate was sold off, or to raise funds to pay debts. Some owners saw their female slaves as brood mares and the children as livestock. Jefferson's assessment of his slaves' value shows his business smarts, but on a human level, it is chilling: "I consider a woman who brings a child every two years as more profitable than the best man of the farm. What she produces is an addition to the capital, while his labors disappear in mere consumption."[i]

If transported slaves were lucky, they were shipped with others of their own ethnic group. But they might just as easily be with other enslaved people who shared no common language and had different customs. This happened to Olaudah Equiano, who was a new African arrival among English-speaking slaves in Virginia: "They could talk to each other, but I had no person to speak to that I could understand."[ii]

The Colston Statue

European ports that relied on the triangular trade included Nantes (France), Liverpool, and Bristol. Slave traders such as Edward Colston, in Bristol, became rich. Colston was a director of the Royal African Company, which is estimated to have exported as many as 84,000 slaves while he held office.

Colston spent some of his wealth on charitable foundations such as almshouses, hospitals, and schools; he also became a Member of Parliament (MP) for his city, which set up a statue of him. This statue became notorious when it was toppled and pushed into the harbor during Black Lives Matter protests in Bristol in June 2020. The statue is now on display in a museum as part of an exhibit, which also includes placards from the BLM protest. One proposal for its replacement is a statue of Paul Stephenson, one of the leaders of the Bristol Bus Boycott of 1963, which challenged the bus company's refusal to hire people of color as bus drivers or conductors.

Slaves were sold at auction, being inspected like cattle by prospective buyers and sometimes stripped naked; their teeth might be examined or their muscles felt. Adding to this humiliation, they were forced to take on new names and use their master's surname—Schuyler, Menendez,

---

[i] "Thomas Jefferson to John Wayles Eppes, 30 June 1820," National Archives/Founders Online, accessed April 2, 2025, https://founders.archives.gov/documents/Jefferson/03-16-02-0052.

[ii] Equiano, Olaudah, *The Interesting Narrative of the Life of Olaudah Equiano, or Gustavus Vassa, the African* (London, 1789).

Hemings—or to bear the name of their origin, such as Congo or Senegambia. Olaudah Equiano was renamed Gustavus Vassa after a king of Sweden; Phillis Wheatley, the first African American published poet, was named after the ship that brought her and the family that bought her. (She was later manumitted, partly due to the influence of her English readership.)

By the eighteenth century, slavery was considered normal. There was racially based slavery in all the colonies, whether British, French, or Spanish. The Constitution allowed for it in Article One, Section Two, stating that slaves would count as "three-fifths of a person" for the enumeration of population to determine taxes and representation. (This gave the Southern states more power than their free White population would have entitled them to have if slaves were excluded.)

In 1793, the Fugitive Slave Law was enacted. Owners were enabled to cross state lines to recover their "property." Slaves, on the other hand, had no access to the law; they could not own property, make contracts, or even defend themselves against their masters.

The nature of slavery differed in detail across colonies and states. For instance, in New England, slavery was generally lighter in touch, with many slaves living in town as part of families, like White servants. In New York, Pinkster (the Dutch Pentecost) was celebrated as "Negro Election Day," with dancing and banjos and drums. In the Carolinas, on the other hand, many White plantation owners from Barbados arrived to settle the colony, together with their slaves, introducing the plantation system and keeping large numbers of slaves in separate slave quarters.

In Louisiana, French settlers brought both slaves and rice from Africa; the Black population outnumbered the White population in the colony. The Code Noir of 1724 was somewhat more humane than in most British-settled states. It barred the separation of spouses or of children under fourteen from their parents. There were free Blacks in Louisiana, too, but their status was second-class. They were required to show respect to White folks, just as slaves were.

Over the course of the seventeenth and eighteenth centuries, the rights of free African Americans were curtailed. For instance, in 1712, New York barred Black people and mulattos (mixed-race individuals) from owning land. In 1660, they were barred from military service in the state of Connecticut.

It wouldn't be fair to suggest that the whole White population approved of slavery. There was significant opposition to it during the eighteenth century, both in Britain and in the New World. The Quakers and Founding Father Thomas Paine were opposed to it, and several US states legislated to ban slavery. Vermont was the first in 1777, with Pennsylvania, Massachusetts, New Hampshire, Connecticut, Rhode Island, New York, and New Jersey following suit. In 1792, the French Revolution marked the end of slavery in France, though it was reintroduced under Napoleon.

In Britain, common law held that slavery could not exist on British soil. A slave who reached England became free (*Shanley v. Harvey*, 1763). However, there was no law against British citizens continuing to own slaves in the West Indies and America. It wasn't until 1834 that Britain banned slavery throughout its dominions, bringing an end to slavery in the Caribbean.

In the United States, the importation of slaves was prohibited in 1807, but this did not constitute the end of slavery. It simply marked a transition between a system that relied on importing fresh slaves from Africa and a new system that relied on the existing slave population reproducing itself.

The plantation system in the Southern states reached its height in the early and mid-nineteenth century. Coffee, rice, tobacco, indigo, sugar, and cotton were all produced using slave labor. The invention of the cotton gin, which mechanically separates cotton fiber from the seeds, brought huge wealth to plantation owners but required significant slave labor to keep it supplied. Only a quarter of the White population owned slaves, and ownership was highly concentrated on the biggest plantations, where the gang labor system was employed.

The slave codes of various states were based on the idea that slaves were property. The laws should therefore protect the owners of such property against any dangers that slaves might represent. Because slaves were property, not persons, under the law, raping a female slave was treated as a crime against the master, not against the woman.

The system was hugely cruel, despite the sanitized version represented in movies such as *Gone with the Wind*. Slaves were often whipped, and female slaves were often sexually abused by White overseers. Masters could beat or even kill their slaves with impunity. Many African American women bore children to their owners. Sally

Hemings, Jefferson's slave, was the mother of his "shadow family." (He freed their four surviving children—two during his life and two in his will.)

But plantation life also enabled African Americans to retain distinctive African customs and culture to a far greater extent than in the North. They lived together on plantation units like village communities, often building their own housing rather than living within a White household. Dancing and music developed out of African traditions, with the "ring shout" (a shuffling circle dance) becoming part of religious ceremonies and the "spiritual" developing as a song form that complained of injustice but looked forward to eventual freedom. African Americans started to build a collective identity of their own.

Quilt making also became a traditional activity among African American women. By making quilts, they could transform waste materials into useful items. Some women sold their quilts, saving up the money they received to buy their freedom. Harriet Powers became famed for her quilts in the 1870s and is considered the mother of the African American story quilt.

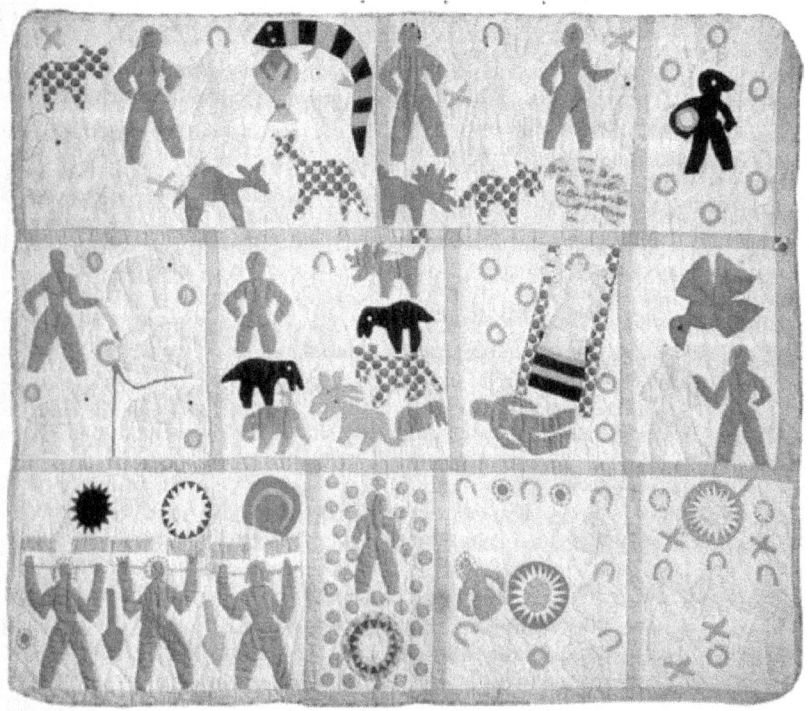

Harriet Powers's Bible quilt. [8]

The American Revolution is a fraught subject when seen in the context of slavery. The rhetoric of the colonies' "enslavement" to Britain and the necessity of freedom applied only to White colonists, not to African Americans. Patrick Henry cried "Give me liberty, or give me death," but in fact, he was a slave owner. Frederick Douglass, escaped slave and abolitionist, asked "What to a Slave is the Fourth of July?"[i]

Even so, several African Americans played a part in the rebellion. For instance, Crispus Attucks was buried with honors after he was killed in the Boston Massacre in 1770. Despite laws officially barring Black people from service in some states, 5,000 of 200,000 soldiers were African American.[ii] Peter Salem and Salem Poor were the heroes of Bunker Hill, and Prince Estabrook fought at Lexington. James Armistead Lafayette worked as a spy for the Marquis de Lafayette (from whom he took his name), penetrating the British camp. Lafayette seconded his plea for emancipation after the war, and the former slave received a pension as well as his freedom.

Washington had originally rejected Black soldiers in 1775. However, when the British offered freedom to any slave prepared to join them, he had to reconsider. (In fact, the British promise was soon broken. When Cornwallis was forced to retreat to Virginia, he refused to take the fugitives with him.) Soon, the Americans were recruiting free Black men and enlisting slaves with a promise of eventual freedom—except in Georgia and South Carolina, which continued to reject Black soldiers outright.

Some Black individuals did well for themselves in the early years of the republic. Captain Absalom F. Boston, son of a freed man, crewed his whaling ship, the *Industry*, exclusively with other Black crewmen, sailing from Nantucket. Prince Hall, founder of the African Masonic Lodge in Boston, owned his own home and a leather working shop. But these were the exceptions, and mainly in the North. While Virginia in 1790 had 13,000 free Black citizens, 96 percent of all Black Virginian were slaves.[iii]

---

[i] Frederick Douglass, "What to a Slave is the Fourth of July?" Speech, July 5, 1852, The Ashbrook Center, accessed April 2, 2025, https://teachingamericanhistory.org/document/what-to-the-slave-is-the-fourth-of-july-4/.

[ii] Franklin and Higginbotham, *From Slavery to Freedom*, 93.

[iii] Franklin and Higginbotham, *From Slavery to Freedom*, 105.

In these early years, there was a property qualification for the right to vote. African Americans who had property could vote. However, when property qualifications were ended, the vote was given only to free White male citizens. By the 1840s, Black citizens almost everywhere had lost their right to vote. In Pennsylvania, William Fogg decided to fight in the courts for his vote: in *Hobbs v. Fogg*, 1837, the Penn Supreme Court held that "a free negro or mulatto is not a citizen within the meaning of the Constitution."

There were also economic reversals for many free Black men, stemming from the fact that immigration from Europe had markedly increased after 1840. Irish and German immigrants now provided a supply of cheap labor in competition with African American employees and businesses.

Slaves did not all accept their fate. There were several slave rebellions during the early nineteenth century. In 1800, slaves marched on Richmond, Virginia, in what became known as Gabriel's Rebellion. However, stormy weather prevented them from gaining their objective, and their plans were discovered. They were rounded up, and their leader, Gabriel, was executed along with thirty-four other slaves.

In 1822, Denmark Vesey modeled his own revolt after Haiti's 1791 slave revolt under Toussaint L'Ouverture. He had bought his freedom with money he won in the Charleston lottery and intended to use it to free other slaves. He was a carpenter, and most of his men were skilled slaves. The African conjurer Gullah Jack was his second in command. The objective was to take over the state armory and give the slaves weapons. However, as with Gabriel's Rebellion, Vesey's plans were leaked to the authorities, and the revolt failed. Forty-seven slaves, including Vesey himself, were executed.

In 1831, during Nat Turner's revolt in Southampton County, Virginia, more than sixty White people were killed. Turner killed his owner's family first. However, state and federal troops killed more than one hundred slaves while putting down the revolt, and Turner was executed. Each of these revolts served as an excuse for even greater repression and violent reprisals. Not only did they not succeed in freeing slaves, but they had the unintended effect of making life even more difficult for African Americans.

In 1838, an interesting legal case created a cause célèbre for abolitionists. The African slaves on the *Amistad*, a Spanish slaver headed for Cuba, rebelled and took over the ship. The Spanish navigator, told by the Africans to sail south, instead surreptitiously steered the ship toward the United States, hoping to be intercepted. Lieutenant Thomas Gedney of the US Navy spotted the ship. He boarded and headed toward Connecticut, which at this time was still a slave state. He intended to claim the slaves as salvage. However, his claim failed.

The Africans were charged with piracy and murder. Abolitionists claimed that they had acted in legitimate self-defense; however, slaves could not claim self-defense. Their legal standing, therefore, would determine their fate. They were represented in court by former president John Quincy Adams, who argued that they were free by natural law. The *Amistad* captives were acquitted and freed. However, in an uneasy compromise, the Supreme Court did not agree that they were naturally free. Instead, the case turned on a technicality. Since the importation of slaves to Cuba was illegal, the Spanish could not prove their ownership. The men were, therefore, not slaves but free men and entitled to act in their own defense.

The uneasy compromise between free (Northern) states and slave (Southern) states was tested several times during the mid-nineteenth century. For instance, when Kansas joined the Union, views differed on whether it should join as a free state or a slave state. This led to violent strife between 1854 and 1859, known as "Bleeding Kansas." Eventually, Kansas joined as a free state.

In 1857, the US Supreme Court ruled that the enslaved Dred Scott had no right to sue for his freedom (*Dred Scott v. Sandford*, known as the Dred Scott Decision). Scott had moved with his master to a free state and claimed his freedom based on his residence there. However, Chief Justice Roger Taney ruled that people of African descent were not included under the word "citizens" in the Constitution, so Scott did not have the standing to file a suit. He also ruled the Missouri Compromise, which prohibited slavery in states north of the 36°30' parallel, unconstitutional, claiming that it interfered with slave owners' property rights (guaranteed by the Fifth Amendment).

This decision has often been considered the single worst decision the Supreme Court has ever made. (Two justices, Benjamin Robbins Curtis and John McLean, dissented.)

Even free Black citizens had a hard time in the early nineteenth century. They had no right to vote and received no protection from the federal government. Further, their access to education and employment was unequal to that enjoyed by White citizens. Southern states passed laws that either prohibited free Black people from settling, required that them to show proof of their freedom, or made them post a bond in order to reside in the state. Harassment occurred in the North as well, but at least in free states, African Americans could assemble to protest for their rights. They could also exercise professions, create institutions for the Black community, and own land. The fear of being enslaved, always present in the South, was not so vivid in the North.

In the past, the abolition of slavery was often portrayed as a gift from the White population to the enslaved Black population. In fact, African Americans played a major role in the abolitionist movement. Frederick Douglass, an escaped slave and fervent abolitionist, used his own experience as fuel for his oratory and traveled to Ireland and Britain, where his lectures were hugely popular. (In fact, it was his British supporters who made him free de jure as well as de facto, buying out his former master.)

Many African Americans were involved in the Underground Railroad, a network of routes, helpers, and safe houses that helped fugitive slaves from the South escape to the free states in the North. This movement had already started in Philadelphia by the late 1790s and gradually spread to other states. Over 3,200 active workers helped a huge number of slaves escape. Governor John Quitman of Mississippi claimed that from 1810 to 1850, over 100,000 slaves had taken the railroad, and that figure may have risen to as much as half a million by the end of the Civil War.

One fascinating "passenger" was Henry "Box" Brown, who mailed himself to freedom in 1847. Packed in a wooden crate, he was freighted from Virginia to the members of the Vigilance Committee Philadelphia, where he was unboxed. He became a major speaker on the abolitionist lecture circuit and toured Britain with an anti-slavery panorama, performing magic tricks.

Harriet Tubman was one of the greatest "conductors." Herself an escaped slave, she made numerous trips to the South and freed many slaves. (There is more about Harriet Tubman in Chapter 7.) Other African Americans participated in running the railroad, too. For instance, Thomas Downing, the African American owner of an oyster bar in New York who became highly wealthy as a result of taking the oyster trade upmarket, used his restaurant as a station on the Underground Railroad. William Still, a free Black man in Philadelphia, was responsible for hundreds of slaves escaping, and eventually published *The Underground Railroad: Authentic Narratives and First-Hand Accounts*.

However, because the railroad was designed to minimize the chances of betrayal, with many of its agents, "station masters," and "conductors" only knowing their own small part of the operation, we'll never know the names of many of the heroic individuals who helped slaves to freedom. We should also remember that it took immense courage for slaves to consider escaping since, if they were caught, they would face considerable penalties.

In the 1850s, there was some interest in returning African Americans to Africa. Some African Americans believed they could never live a worthwhile life in a country run by White men. Others, though, pointed out that America was now their home. By this stage, most slaves, other than the very oldest, had been born in the United States. Some Black people also investigated emigration to Canada (where the Fugitive Slave Law did not apply) or Haiti, and many prominent escaped slaves (like "Box" Brown) decided that Britain was safer for them than the US. However, Southern White folks found the establishment of Liberia an intriguing way of getting rid of free Black citizens—regarded as a nuisance since they did not contribute to the plantation economy. They pledged their full support to the venture.

Owen Brown, an abolitionist, had supported Oberlin College (which admitted African Americans from 1835) and was active in the Underground Railroad. Brown was principled and well connected. He refused to assist local White families in driving off Native Americans who had hunting grounds in the area, and he knew Frederick Douglass and Sojourner Truth. His son, John Brown, had been involved in Bleeding Kansas, and as politics became more polarized, he decided that peaceful action (as espoused by his father) was no longer enough.

In 1859, he and his followers planned to take the Harper's Ferry arsenal in Virginia, with the aim of giving the weapons to a slave rebellion. His attempt on Harper's Ferry failed, and he was hanged for treason against the state of Virginia. But his sincere Christian faith displayed throughout his trial won him great admiration. With his last words, he seems to have predicted the Civil War: "I, John Brown, am now quite certain that the crimes of this guilty land will never be purged away but with blood."[i]

The action at Harper's Ferry, though failing its avowed purpose, played an important part in ending slavery, since it increased the polarization of American politics between Southern slave-owning interests and an increasingly abolitionist North.

The last straw for the uneasy compromise between slave states and free states was the election of Lincoln in 1860. Lincoln's view was that the Union should no longer admit slave states; any states that joined in future would have to be free states. Faced with what they considered an abolitionist president, South Carolina seceded in December 1860, and ten further states joined the Confederacy in 1861. The Civil War had begun.

The 1862 Emancipation Proclamation was a psychologically important moment from which there was no going back. It promised freedom to all slaves in Confederate-held states. This was politically smart as well as principled. It undermined the basis of the Southern plantation economy and made support from Europe unlikely since no French or British government would want to be seen actively supporting slavery. However, it was also neatly limited in effect. As a concession to the buffer states—Kentucky, Maryland, Missouri, and Delaware—it did not apply to areas that were already under Union control.

Many African Americans were participants in their own liberation. Though the Union forces were segregated, 200,000 African American volunteers served in the Civil War, and in fact, the war could not have been won without them. There were 144 Black infantry regiments, fourteen artillery regiments and seven cavalry regiments. Frederick Douglass' sons served in the 54th Massachusetts. In 1864, equal pay and conditions for African American troops were agreed to.

At Fort Pillow, Union forces were overwhelmed by the Confederates, who proceeded to shoot down soldiers who surrendered, the African Americans because of their race and the White soldiers because they "fought with n----s." Fort Pillow become a battle cry for the Union.

---

[i] "John Brown's Holy War: The Hanging," WGBH Educational Foundation. Accessed April 2, 2025. https://www.pbs.org/wgbh/americanexperience/features/brown-hanging/.

Among heroes of the Civil War, thirty-seven African Americans in the armed forces won Medals of Honor, and Harriet Tubman served as a scout, nurse, and cook. (She also led an attack on rice plantations in South Carolina and freed 800 slaves.) Robert Smalls, a slave pilot who worked in the Charleston shipyards, took control of the Confederate steamer *Planter* and handed it over to the Union Navy.

The end of the Civil War in 1865 brought a series of amendments to the Constitution:

- The Thirteenth Amendment (1865), which outlawed slavery
- The Fourteenth Amendment (1868), which forbade states from denying any American citizen the equal protection of the law
- The Fifteenth Amendment (1870), which guarantees the right to vote regardless of race, color, or previous enslavement

African Americans were now free and equal—at least in theory. But, as the next chapter will tell, theory and practice were two different things.

Chapter 2: The Struggle for Civil Rights Post Civil-War

The years of Reconstruction started off well for African Americans. They had gained their freedom and a political voice, and in the 1870s, Southern Black citizens used their votes. It was the Republican Party that rallied Black votes through the Union League, and quite effectively. Several Black men achieved elected office. In South Carolina, the first legislature of Reconstruction saw eighty-seven Black and forty White officials elected. There were Black speakers of the house and lieutenant governors (though never a Black governor). Forty Black members were elected in Mississippi, including former slaves. Black

During the debates over the 1875 Civil Rights Act, the former Confederacy vice-president Alexander Stephens spoke against the act in the House of Representatives; he was rebutted by the Black congressman Robert Brown Elliott.

On a personal level, many former slaves searched for the families from which they had been separated, and some found them. Others were able to regularize their marriages, which had not been officially recognized while they were enslaved. They also started to work for their future, setting up schools and colleges. Some communities even raised money to employ their own teachers. Freedmen put a huge emphasis on education, which would complete the work begun by the emancipation of the slaves.

The Freedmen's Bureau, which was America's first major welfare program, worked with philanthropic and religious organizations to set up regular schools, night schools, colleges, and industrial schools. It must have been a particularly sweet revenge for many African Americans to see schools set up in the buildings of former slave markets, such as the Bryan Free School in Savannah, particularly since the proceeds of slavery had funded many educational institutions such as Harvard, Princeton, and Yale.

This period also saw the foundation of Howard University and Atlanta University specifically for African American students. It is no coincidence that Howard now has a reputable Black history department. It is now ranked in the top hundred American universities.

However, White interests in the South clawed back much of what had been won through a variety of means, ranging from legal cases to outright terrorism. The economic as well as legal emancipation of former slaves had originally been envisaged as a form of land reform which would have distributed abandoned land to freedmen and refugees. Instead, it was sold off to wealthy (and usually White) owners.

Sharecropping, created in the late 1860s, initially seemed to offer African Americans the freedom to manage their own smallholdings, with the right to a proportion of the harvested crop from the land. However, things did not work out that way. Wealthy planters tied the sharecropping families into supply contracts for machinery, seed, tools and fertilizer, putting many of them into debt. The Freedman's Bank, which opened in 1865, offered another chance, but was unfortunately used by some unscrupulous financiers as a place to get rid of their bad loans. Although Frederick Douglass took over and attempted to save it, the bank failed in 1874. Thus, African Americans generally remained at an economic disadvantage.

A rearguard action was being fought over emancipation. For instance, the Fourteenth Amendment (which guaranteed equal access to the law for all citizens) was held to apply only to federal issues, not state-level rights. This meant that, while an African American citizen might have certain theoretical rights, the state in which he lived could limit his rights in certain ways with impunity—keeping Black citizens "in their place."

Numerous state laws constrained Black citizens. "Public order" was White order—that is, the absence of Black folks from the public sphere, whether transportation or politics. As the (White) Louisiana journalist

George W. Cable wrote in *The Negro Question (1890)*, "Any colored man gains unquestioned admission into innumerable places the moment he appears as the menial attendant of some White person, where he could not cross the threshold in his own right as well-dressed and well-behaved master of himself."[i]

The Democratic Party took back the South in a vote for White "home rule"—anti-Black, anti-Yankee, and anti-Republican. Legal as well as political reverses piled up. In 1883, the Supreme Court ruled the 1875 Civil Rights Act unconstitutional, stating that while the government could legislate for the states, it could not tell individuals or businesses how to act.

The Jim Crow laws—named after a minstrel character—established racial segregation in most states, not just in the South. Racial segregation was evident in education, sport, health, transport, entertainment, and even in the prohibition of interracial marriage. Restaurants and cinemas barred Black patrons, while some institutions had separate entrances for them.

The 1890 Louisiana Comfort of Passengers Act mandated segregated railroad travel. In 1896, the Black community decided to bring a test case, *Plessy v. Ferguson*, choosing a passenger who was seven-eighths White and could pass for White. Homer Plessy lost his case. The Supreme Court decided that "separate but equal" facilities could be provided, effectively authorizing a form of apartheid in America. Of course, the facilities provided for White and African American citizens were never quite equal, but even so, the case wasn't overturned until 1954.

The rationale for the *Plessy v. Ferguson* decision was that "If one race be inferior to the other socially, the Constitution of the United States cannot put them on the same plane." In other words, having suffered enslavement, African Americans should continue to suffer the economic, social, and educational disadvantages that accrued to them as a result.[ii]

This decision effectively institutionalized economic and social inequality. Only John Marshall Harlan, known as "The Great Dissenter" for his refusal to limit civil rights, dissented in this case. (His grandson,

---

[i] Franklin and Higginbotham, *From Freedom to Slavery*, 271.

[ii] "Plessy v. Ferguson (1896)," National Archives, updated February 8, 2022. https://www.archives.gov/milestone-documents/plessy-v-ferguson.

also John Marshall Harlan, likewise sat on the Supreme Court and, while generally conservative, strongly supported civil rights.)

If *Plessy v. Ferguson* was a disaster, *Cumming v. County Board of Education* (1899) was even worse; it enabled segregated education even when there was no provision made at all for Black students.

Of course, African Americans had the vote, but it was made more and more difficult to exercise that freedom. For instance, many states introduced rules that included tests of literacy or knowledge of the Constitution. Failure to pay tax was also found to be a disqualifying factor. Election districts gerrymandered to put the Black vote in a minority in as many districts as possible. The state of Louisiana also introduced a "grandfather clauses" that stated only those whose fathers and grandfathers were qualified to vote in 1867 could do so. Of course, 1867 was before the Fifteenth Amendment, so that ruled out most Black voters.

Completely illegal means to deter the Black vote were also used. Some planters told their Black sharecroppers how to vote, while polling stations were often set up only in majority-White areas or unexpectedly moved on polling day. Black citizens were often run out of town at election time, and ballot boxes were "stuffed." The Democratic Party in the South held "White primaries." Since the Democrat candidate would win any general election, this effectively disenfranchised Black voters.

While this was mainly a problem in the South, the North was complicit. In 1877, Republican presidential candidate Rutherford B. Hayes lost the popular vote but reached a deal with three Southern states to gain control of the electoral college. He withdrew federal troops from the South and ended federal support for Reconstruction. This effectively gave the new (White) ruling class in the South carte blanche.

Vigilante action against African Americans became common. The Ku Klux Klan was not the only group or even the most influential. There were the Knights of the White Camelia, the Red Shirts, and the White League. White supremacists aimed to retain control through terror, massacres, staged riots, and intimidation of African American voters by armed patrols. The vigilantes, together with the increasing legal difficulties put in the way of Black voters, managed to eradicate the Republican and Black vote in the South almost completely.

In 1868, more than 200 African Americans were killed in the Opelousas Massacre in Louisiana. Emerson Bentley, a White schoolteacher and newspaper editor, was attacked by White supremacists while teaching a classroom of Black schoolchildren. False rumors of his death led Black Republicans to threaten revenge, but they were heavily outnumbered. Over the course of several weeks, Black citizens were harassed, shot, and killed. Between 150 and 300 African Americans were killed, while the Freedmen's School was destroyed, as was the office of Bentley's newspaper, *The St. Landry Progress*. This effectively eliminated the Republican Party in the area.

Another dreadful event was the Thibodaux Massacre of 1887. Ten thousand sugar cane workers, nine-tenths of whom were Black, had gone on strike during the harvest, protesting their working conditions. The violence began with a White man entering a Black-owned bar and shooting two Black workers (killing one); it then escalated. Somewhere between thirty and fifty African Americans were killed, while many more were wounded or went missing (possibly fleeing to other areas).

Racial violence included lynchings, which White supremacists used as a means of social control. There were at least 2,500 lynchings from 1894 to 1900 and another thousand before the First World War, in the Midwest as well as the South. They were rarer (though not unknown) in the Northern states. Race riots occurred across the US. In just a few years, at the start of the twentieth century, there were three serious riots:

- The 1904 riot in Springfield, Ohio

    An African American was lynched after being jailed for shooting a White officer. After the lynching, the crowd went on the rampage, assaulting Black citizens and burning their houses.

- The 1908 riot in Springfield, Illinois

    After a Black man who had been accused of raping a White woman had been removed to another town as a precautionary measure, White citizens rioted. The militia was called out. African American houses and businesses were destroyed, a Black barber was lynched, and an eighty-four-year-old Black man married to a White woman was also lynched.

- The 1906 riot in Atlanta, Georgia

    Houses of Black citizens were looted and torched for several days, and African Americans were attacked on the street. The Atlanta Civic League was formed to improve social conditions, but no one was ever punished for the riots.

Although racial violence was widespread, the situation was undoubtedly much worse in the Southern states. This led to an exodus of African Americans. In the 1870s, many moved to Texas, Kansas, and the West. From the 1890s onward, many migrated north, as well as to California and Colorado. Then, from 1914 to 1929, up to a million African Americas resettled in Northern states in what is known as the Great Migration. This pattern continued after the Second World War, with another three million moving north during the 1950s, '60s and '70s. Many moved to Chicago and other large cities in the Northeast and Midwest. Chicago was a particularly attractive destination, with its outspoken Black-owned newspaper *The Chicago Defender*, which campaigned against racial abuse and discrimination. More than half its readership was outside Chicago.

Part of the reason for the exodus was the Jim Crow laws. But there was also the fact that the South was no longer as wealthy as it had been. Small farmers had been driven off the land by the increasing mechanization of the larger estates and the boll weevil infestation of 1915. Compared to this, the North had industrialized and was experiencing a high demand for labor.

Alongside migration came a major change in lifestyle. African Americans were moving out of rural areas and agricultural-related jobs and into cities and factory work. Cities such as New Orleans, Atlanta, Charleston, and Savannah saw huge increases in their Black populations.

There were, of course, some downsides to urban life. Jobs were often segregated, with the more skilled and highly paid crafts reserved for White workers. In Philadelphia, for instance, bricklayers were White, but Black men were hired as their hod carriers. Most trades unions did not accept Black workers, so they had relatively little labor power. Cities also attempted to segregate Black residents into particular residential areas. This was the norm even in the North, and race riots were part of the urban landscape.

This period spurred the development of Black culture, in which the Baptist Church formed a strong focus. One of the principal leaders of this movement was Richard Allen, a freedman (who had bought his brother's freedom alongside his own). Excluded by the White worshipers at the Episcopal church in Philadelphia, he decided to found his own church, the African Methodist Episcopal Church. It brought a potent message of betterment for African Africans through spiritual progress. This blend of spirituality and civic discourse became characteristic of the African American community, and it is from this background that Martin Luther King Jr. emerged to lead the civil rights movement.

Peter Williams, founder of the African Methodist Episcopal Zion Church, also started his church as a response to exclusion. The trustees of his church had raised the funds to buy his freedom but made Black members sit at the back of the church—the epitome of White people's mixed feelings about Black emancipation. (Many White Christians quoted Noah's curse on his grandson Ham in Genesis 8:25-27 to justify their view of Black people as racially inferior: "And he said, Cursed be Canaan; a servant of servants shall he be unto his brethren.")

Pentecostalism, with its speaking in tongues and fervent, direct experience of the Holy Spirit, particularly appealed to the Black community. In Los Angeles, William J. Seymour's Azusa Street Revival of 1906 onward was crucial in the widespread growth of Pentecostalism throughout the early twentieth century.

Since African Americans could not at that time play a major role in electoral politics and were not admitted to most trade unions, the church was their main way of influencing public discourse and representing themselves. They also set up community institutions. In the North, free African Americans had set up several early societies such as the Free African Society of Newport, Rhode Island (1780) and the African Society in Boston (1796). Boston's African Americans set up a school for Black students.

Booker T. Washington was an immensely influential African American writer, intellectual, and educator. He founded the Tuskegee Institute in 1881 to deliver industrial and craft training and build African American self-sufficiency. It was his belief that economic parity would have to be achieved before social parity became possible.

Many White Americans found his willingness to accept the racial status quo "for the time being" attractive, and he was patronized by Andrew Carnegie, Julius Rosenwald, John D. Rockefeller, William Howard Taft, and others. At Tuskegee, he tried hard to avoid antagonizing White Southerners with the line that the education of Black folks was in their own interests. It was a highly practical program of self-sufficiency, including the mule-drawn "Movable School" for Tuskegee's agricultural outreach program, which helped increase the productivity of Black-owned farms.

When Booker T. Washington was invited to dine at the White House with President Roosevelt, Southerners were aghast at this breach of etiquette. But he was no Uncle Tom. Frequently, though secretly, he funded test cases against segregation. He was not a separatist but simply believed that fighting for economic self-sufficiency first was the correct way to proceed. He looked forward to the eventual full integration of African Americans into the life of the nation.

The 1890s saw African Americans wanting more control in institutions such as Fisk and Howard universities. Howard University passed over John Mercer Langston, the African American founding dean of its law school, as permanent president of the school. This led to some Black separatists saying it was time to go it alone.

On the other hand, some African Americans believed that social equality had to be achieved at all costs. W.E.B. Du Bois founded the Niagara Movement in 1905, which was dedicated to the abolition of all racial discrimination. In 1910, the National Association for the Advancement of Colored People (NAACP) was founded, absorbing the Niagara Movement. W.E.B. Du Bois became the editor of its news magazine, *The Crisis*. The NAACP united African Americans and White allies who opposed racist laws. By 1911, it had chapters in Chicago, Boston, and New York.

The Declaration of Principles of the Niagara Movement includes a stirring call to action: "The voice of protest of ten million Americans must never cease to assail the ears of their fellows, so long as America is unjust."[i] This call to action would continue to inspire the NAACP and the civil rights movement for decades to come.

W.E.B. Du Bois believed that African Americans needed access to the arts and humanities, not just to industrial and crafts training. Du Bois had attended Fisk University, then Harvard (where he took a PhD in history), and also studied in Berlin. He rejected Booker T. Washington's conciliatory attitude to the racist South. Without an

---

[i] "Niagara's Declaration of Principles, 1905," MacMillan Center for International and Area Studies at Yale, accessed April 2, 2025. https://macmillan.yale.edu/glc/niagaras-declaration-principles-1905.

effective vote and social equality, he did not believe African Americans would ever achieve economic parity.

Du Bois developed the concept of double consciousness in his 1903 work *The Souls of Black Folk*. According to him, African Americans were both American and Negro. They experienced the difficulty of having to look at themselves through the eyes of a racist White society, needing to reconcile their African roots with the European-dominated world in which they were brought up. But he also advocated that African Americans needed to become a people with pride in themselves and their culture.

Both Washington and Du Bois, however different their strategies, looked forward to integration and equality. Marcus Garvey, on the other hand, advocated full scale separatism with his "Back to Africa" vision. He believed that Black folks needed to live in a majority Black society to succeed.

Originally from Jamaica, Garvey became controversial in the US for his separatist views and his talks with leaders of the Ku Klux Klan (KKK). He despised Jews and mixed-race people and asserted that the NAACP really wanted African Americans to become White. Compared with Du Bois' rather Ivy League appeal, his views appealed more to the Black working class who were becoming disillusioned with the lack of progress.

Despite his controversial views, Garvey helped to create a huge Afrocentric drive for racial pride, which later influenced movements as diverse as the Nation of Islam, Rastafari, and Black Power.

He was ultimately prosecuted for mail fraud (he had quite possibly been framed) and deported from the US; he died in London.

The defining achievement of this period was the creation of a nationwide movement for the advancement of African Americans. Though Washington, Du Bois and Garvey had very different views, all of them asserted Black pride and aspiration. The stage was now set for the Harlem Renaissance and its concept of the "New Negro."

Chapter 3: The Harlem Renaissance

The various migrations from the South had brought new African American residents to the Northern cities. At the same time, W.E.B. Du Bois and Booker T. Washington had helped generate a lively, nationwide movement of Black advancement. The investment in educational facilities for African Americans during Reconstruction had created a generation of well-educated and articulate Negros (the term used at the time). These developments came together most notably in the Harlem Renaissance. This chapter will look at this sudden explosion of African American arts, music, and literature.

A Tale of Two Cities

There are two cities that are prominent in this chapter. One is, obviously, New York. The other is Paris, France. Many Americans went to Paris during the 1920s and 1930s—famously, Ezra Pound, Ernest Hemingway, Scott Fitzgerald, and Henry Miller, but also African Americans Ella Fitzgerald, Langston Hughes, Josephine Baker, and Richard Wright. Josephine Baker moved to France and found it so much to her taste that she never moved back, and several other African Americans decided to stay long term.

Paris enriched African Americans by showing them a society with no segregated bars and introducing them to Francophone Black intellectuals like Léopold Sédar

Senghor and Aimé Césaire, who were developing the concept of "negritude." African Americans had contact with Black French people from the Caribbean and West Africa (Senghor eventually became the first president of Senegal), the first time most had directly experienced African culture.

In 1921, France's premier literary prize, the Prix Goncourt, was awarded to the Martinique-born Black writer René Maran for his novel *Batouala*. African Americans were amazed. Not only had the prize gone to a Black writer (a Pulitzer wouldn't go to a Black American writer until 1950), but the Goncourt had been awarded to a book that didn't pull its punches when discussing racism and colonialism. The award neatly shows the differences between the French Negro experience and that of African American intellectuals.

Paris was also one of the great centers of jazz—possibly brought there by the Harlem Hellfighters (a Black regiment) in the First World War. It witnessed the continual interchange of jazz musicians and musical trends between France and the United States, welcoming Black musicians such as Louis Armstrong, Sidney Bechet, Duke Ellington, and Ella Fitzgerald.

In New York, a sort of "Black Bohemia" started in the Tenderloin, on the West Side, where African American actors, writers, and other artists came together to live close to the theater district. The Tenderloin was also a high crime district. Eventually, many of the wealthier African American inhabitants of the area moved farther north to Harlem. By the 1920s, it had become a sought-out center of entertainment, with many cabarets, speakeasies, and literary coteries.

It was here the Harlem Renaissance began. There were several important factors at play: increasingly high educational levels in the urban African American population, the economic boom of the early 1920s, the advent of modernism as an artistic movement, the creation of mass entertainment, and the spread of radio and the phonograph. At the same time, many White artists were becoming interested in "primitive" (African) art, creating an openness to artistic creations that were not in the European tradition.

Alain Locke studied at Harvard, Oxford, and Berlin and taught at Howard University. In 1925, he contributed five essays to the collection *The New Negro*, which he also edited. (The same year, he was dismissed after demanding equal pay for Black and White faculty but was reinstated the next year by Howard's first African American president, Mordecai W. Johnson.)

The concept of the "New Negro" was key to the Harlem Renaissance. Ethnic pride helped create a new Black identity by bringing the African American experience into mainstream American culture. According to Locke, race was built, not inborn; it was a cultural creation. The New Negro would no longer allow White people to define him or her but would take power for himself or herself.

Locke's ideas were taken up by a generation of writers like Zora Neale Hurston, whose novels mainly focus on the African American experience—particularly that of African American women. Hurston's *Their Eyes Were Watching God*, published in 1937, tells the story of Janie Crawford, granddaughter of an enslaved woman, child of rape, and survivor of two loveless marriages. The novel portrays the objectification and domination of African American women by men, as well as one woman's search for her own voice. Earlier Black narratives had often been focused on escape from slavery, such as Olaudah Equiano's and Frederick Douglass's autobiographies. But, for the first time, an African American woman's struggle for her identity was made the basis of the story.

Langston Hughes was another star of the Harlem Renaissance, a prolific writer in several different genres. He was also a wanderer, making his way to Mexico and Africa as well as Europe. He even crewed on board the S.S. *Malone* for six months, though he eventually settled down in Harlem. (Travels to Russia, Central Asia, Japan, China and Korea followed, but he always came back to Harlem.)

The NAACP newsletter *The Crisis* published a great number of his poems. The ongoing struggle for African American rights and the promotion of African American writers and artists were strongly related at this time. Hughes made working-class Black people his subject, a very different emphasis from the rather middle-class world of W.E.B. Du Bois. In *The Weary Blues* (1926), he used jazz and blues rhythms in his poetry, linking it to the music that was identified with African Americans and had come up from the South.

While earlier African American writers had often been careful to manage their impact on White readers, Hughes was no longer concerned with what a White public might think. "We younger Negro artists who create now intend to express our individual dark-skinned selves without fear or shame," he said.[i] His poems reflect a great pride in his race, completely free of the desire to pass for White or copy European-style culture.

Hughes had an important part to play in the Harlem Renaissance. He was always helping other writers, editing collections, introducing writers to publishers, and working within arts organizations. The Harlem Renaissance was very much a communal effort.

Harlem had a vibrant nightlife, and this contributed to the cultural ferment of the times. White writer Ridgely Torrence had helped kick things off back in 1917 by penning plays for Black actors that let them play real roles instead of being limited to blackface/minstrel stereotypes. The Lafayette Players, Harlem's first Black theater company, pioneered African American Shakespeare and other serious works; it also gave Dooley Wilson ("Sam" in *Casablanca*) his start in show business. In 1924, Paul Robeson starred in Eugene O'Neill's play *All God's Chillun Got Wings*—the first time a Black man played the lead role opposite a White woman. (Later, Robeson would be the first African American to star in a Hollywood film as Brutus in *The Emperor Jones* and would play Shakespeare's Black hero Othello.)

There were several Black musicals, such as *Shuffle Along* on Broadway, and Harlem was the focus of the jazz scene in New York. Harlem stride piano was the local style, adding piano to the Southern brass band mix. Great names of the day included Jelly Roll Morton (born Ferdinand Joseph LaMothe), Fats Waller, and Duke Ellington. In 1920, Mamie Smith was the first African American woman to record the blues. Her *Crazy Blues* sold 75,000 copies in Harlem, proving there was a market for African American voices and opening this market for other Black singers.

In the fashion world, European influences were suffused with African vibes. Bold colors and strong patterns were used, with a stress on refinement. Flapper dresses were common, while men wore highly tailored suits with fedora hats. This era saw the beginnings of the zoot suit (a loose fitting suit with a long jacket), though it didn't reach its heyday until the 1940s. Flamboyance and confidence were essential characteristics of the style.

---

[i] Franklin and Higginbotham, *From Slavery to Freedom*, 413.

James Van Der Zee set up his photography studio in Harlem in 1916, and his photographs record the life of Harlem's ordinary people as well as the trendsetters. He lived well into his nineties and, in 1982, photographed the young painter Jean Michel Basquiat for *Interview* magazine. His images of modern Black life contrast with the Hollywood stereotypes like "Mammy," played by Hattie McDaniel in *Gone with the Wind*, and Lincoln Perry's "Stepin Fetchit."

In Harlem Renaissance art, modernist and African influences mixed to create vibrant and colorful styles. Aaron Douglas developed a style that uses human silhouettes within patterned layers of landscape or abstraction to convey a forceful emotional impact. He adopted methods from cubism but also refers to African dancing and masks in his work. He created murals at the Harlem nightclub Ebony and illustrated articles in *The Crisis* and other Black publications. Like many of the Harlem writers and musicians, he spent time in Paris.

Augusta Savage, a native Floridian, ran free classes in the arts and was an important member of the Harlem artistic community, as well as a talented sculptor. Like Douglas, she spent time in Europe, touring Germany and studying in Paris. Her *Lift Every Voice and Sing*, the only work commissioned from an African American for the 1939 New York World's Fair, creates a harp out of human figures, with God's hand holding them as the soundboard. It was named after a hymn that had become an unofficial national anthem for African Americans. However, the exhibition organizers either did not understand or did not approve the message, renaming it *The Harp*.

The Harlem Renaissance was an explosion of freedom, including sexual freedom for women and LGBTQ+ African Americans. Early blues singer Ma Rainey let her bisexuality show through her songs, while Bessie Smith's songs are frank about female sexuality.

The freedom and optimism of the era is perhaps most easy to appreciate through the music of Duke Ellington, who was at the heart of the Harlem Renaissance. After a tough start, his career took off in the mid-1920s, and in 1927, his band was given a regular booking with weekly broadcasts from the Cotton Club (a White-only venue). Duke would go on to take jazz forward for the next five decades and had the ambition of making it comparable to classical music with longer, more complex composed pieces such as *Black, Brown and Beige* (1943).

Chapter 4: The Civil Rights Movement: Heroes, Triumphs and Protests

Half a million African Americans served overseas during the Second World War, like the 761st Tank Battalion—the original "Black Panthers." They arrived in France in September 1944 and fought in Northern France and then Germany, notably in the Battle of the Bulge. Often, they were at the front of the advance into German territory. In 1945, they liberated the Gunskirchen concentration camp. Like many African American achievements, theirs was recognized many years later. Jimmy Carter conferred the Presidential Unit Citation on the 761st in 1978.

African Americans knew what they were fighting for, calling the war the "Double V Campaign." Double victory meant winning victory over fascism in Europe and victory over racism in the United States. In fact, some Black soldiers saw desegregated life for the first time in Europe. In the United Kingdom, many British people were shocked when White US officers tried to enforce segregation in British pubs, and some landlords refused to allow it. African Americans fought the entire war in segregated units. (The end of segregation in the military came in 1947, but the US Army retained some segregated units until 1954.)

When these soldiers returned to the US and found the same discrimination and prejudice as before the war, they determined to do something about it. Membership in the NAACP rose fast. While the NAACP continued its progress in legal and lobbying work, it soon began a new, grassroots style of action, taking the battle for civil rights further.

The great migration had made a major change in the lifestyles of African Americans. During Reconstruction, most African Americans still lived rurally; by the end of the Second World War, most had moved into the cities. The Black population of the ten largest US cities was only 3 percent of their total population in 1900 but had risen to 19 percent in 1950. (That grew to 31 percent in 1990, according to figures from the US Census.)

There had also been some major changes in politics. While during Reconstruction the Republican Party had supported African Americans (and been supported by them in turn), it now decided to target the South, and that meant winning over White voters. In the 1928 presidential election, influential Black newspapers decided to endorse the Democratic candidate instead. The Democratic Party had also changed over time.

Franklin D. Roosevelt's presidency and the New Deal, which created huge public works programs to address the dearth of employment, introduced significant changes for all Americans, specifically for African Americans. Roosevelt had friendly relationships with influential African Americans and set up a "Black Cabinet," or "Black Brain Trust," which broke new ground by including a woman, Mary McLeod Bethune. First Lady Eleanor Roosevelt frequently visited Black schools and community projects.

Black Americans now had significant electoral power in the Northern cities. Oscar De Priest was the first Black alderman in Chicago and entered Congress as representative for Illinois' First District; he was rejected in 1934 in favor of Arthur W. Mitchell, a Black Democrat.

African Americans in the labor force benefited from the expansion of union power, which had begun before WW2. In 1925, Asa Philip Randolph had founded the Brotherhood of Sleeping Car Porters and Maids, which finally won a contract with Pullman, the first ever for an African American union, in 1937. Randolph was a leading figure of the early civil rights movement who lobbied US presidents and worked at a high level for the advancement of his people. (He was one of those who had lobbied for desegregation of the military.)

In 1938, there had been a split between the American Federation of Labor (AFL) and the Committee for Industrial Organizations (CIO), which invited African American participation. (The CIO became the Congress of Industrial Organizations.) The AFL had often been considered protective of White interests. The CIO was organized differently. Its unions were not based on specific skills but on specific employers, so it was able to represent Black workers, who were often kept in unskilled jobs. The United Auto Workers (UAW) was a particularly important union for African Americans, many of whom were employed in auto works in Detroit, and it decided to join the CIO rather than stay with the AFL.

Labor justice was a huge issue from the Depression onward. Unemployment hit everyone but was a particular scourge for African Americans: a quarter of Black men were unemployed. Boycotts of businesses that wouldn't hire African Americans started in Chicago in 1929 and quickly spread to other Northern cities, with the slogan "Don't buy where you can't work." This direct action worked in many cases, and it set a precedent for the direct action campaigns the NAACP would use during the 1940s and 1950s.

In 1947, Jackie Robinson was recruited to the Brooklyn Dodgers, the first time the baseball color bar had been breached. He was a high-profile example of the progress being made, and at his opening game, more than half the spectators were Black. Racist comments from other teams helped unite the Dodgers behind Robinson. Jewish star Hank Greenberg (who had also encountered racism during his career) encouraged him, while teammate Pee Wee Reese said, "You can hate a man for many reasons. Color is not one of them."[i]

(Incidentally, while in the US Army, Jackie Robinson had been court-martialed after refusing to go to the back of a bus even though Army buses were, in theory, desegregated. Although the panel of officers which judged his case was all White, he was acquitted of all charges.)

The NAACP continued to be a major force pushing for change. It grew out of a strong tradition of self-help and the confidence that African Americans had the power and ability to change their future. Individual

---

[i] Rick Morain, "Breaking the Barrier," *Storm Lake Times Pilot*, April 27, 2022, https://www.stormlake.com/stories/breaking-the-barrier,50170.

and collective transformation were linked, as shown in the motto of the National Association of Colored Women's Clubs: "Lifting as we climb."

For the NAACP, the 1940s marked the passing of the old guard and a new focus on empowerment. But it continued its commitment to non-violent protest. The example of Mahatma Gandhi, whose civil disobedience campaign had won Indian independence, showed powerfully how non-violent action could be effective. He was an inspiration to many in the civil rights movement.

In 1948, Truman became the first presidential candidate to campaign in Harlem, and the Black vote was crucial in getting him re-elected. He echoed the Double V Campaign in explicitly linking his liberal civil rights program with the Cold War agenda. "If we wish to inspire the people of the world whose freedom is in jeopardy," he claimed, "we must correct the remaining imperfections in our practice of democracy."[i]

The *Green Book*

The *Negro Motorist Green Book* was a guide for African American motorists, a little like the famed French Michelin guides. But instead of being focused on tourist sites or great gastronomy, the *Green Book* listed establishments on the road and in major cities that would treat African American customers with dignity and respect. The first annual *Green Book* came out in 1936, and it continued to be published until the 1960s.

The scene was now set for the heyday of the civil rights movement in the 1950s. A new style of civil action began in Montgomery, Alabama, in December 1955, when a woman named Rosa Parks refused to give up her seat at the front of the "Black section" of the bus to a White passenger. She was arrested for refusing to obey.

Her action was part of a strategy. She was an NAACP member and knew she was drawing attention to the discriminatory laws in place. Reacting to her arrest, the NAACP called for a boycott of public transport in Montgomery, Alabama, where the incident had taken place.

It was the young Martin Luther King Jr. who led the boycott. He was a recent arrival to Montgomery, where he was well regarded as an inspiring preacher; he was also a pacifist, influenced by Gandhi and

---

[i] Franklin and Higginbotham, *From Slavery to Freedom*, 5537.

writer Henry David Thoreau. In his opening speech to the Montgomery Improvement Association, he said, "We have no alternative but to protest ... we have come here tonight to be saved from the patience that makes us patient with anything less than freedom and justice."[i]

African American maids working in White families were often asked whether they had joined the boycott. With charming duplicity, they often said they'd have nothing to do with any boycott. In fact, the boycott so worried them that they'd just stay away from the buses until it was over.

However, while the boycott dominated the news, the NAACP was still using its legal smarts, too. A class action was brought against the mayor of Montgomery (with Aurelia Browder, not Rosa Parks, as the lead plaintiff), challenging the constitutionality of city and state segregation laws. This action was successful. The US District Court declared Alabama's segregation laws unconstitutional, and this was affirmed by the Supreme Court. Within a little more than a year, the buses were desegregated—a major victory for the civil rights movement.

Education as well as buses became a battleground. In 1957, the Little Rock Nine became a cause célèbre. Arkansas governor Orval Faubus refused to integrate the Central High School in Little Rock, whose student body was all White. He called out the Arkansas National Guard to prevent the admission of nine African American students despite a federal court order to admit them.

In response, President Eisenhower sent in paratroopers and federalized the Arkansas National Guard, bringing it under his direct control and ordering it to support the integration of the school. The message was clear: the federal government was committed to supporting integration, no matter what it took, and states needed to fall into line.

Perhaps the biggest achievement of the civil rights movement in the 1950s was the result of legal action by the NAACP. The strategy of fighting civil rights cases and taking them as far as possible in the courts had been developed by Charles Hamilton Houston in the 1930s. The NAACP fought cases on voting rights, educational integration, equal access to transport and housing, and equal teachers' salaries, accumulating small, steady wins.

---

[i] C. Carson and D.L. Lewis, "Martin Luther King, Jr." *Encyclopedia Britannica*, March 31, 2025. https://www.britannica.com/biography/Martin-Luther-King-Jr/The-Montgomery-bus-boycott.

Houston was joined by his former student Thurgood Marshall, who became legal director of the NAACP. He won two cases for admission to schools in 1950, but they did not overrule the "separate but equal" doctrine of *Plessy*. They simply rejected the offer of inferior educational opportunities to Black students.

But, in 1954, Marshall had the chance he was looking for. In *Brown v. Board of Education of Topeka, Kansas*, he won the unanimous ruling from the Supreme Court that four African American children had to be admitted by the Topeka, Kansas Board of Education. But, more importantly, he finally got *Plessy* overturned.

Everyone knew that "separate but equal" facilities were far from equal in reality. West Memphis, Arkansas, spent $144.51 for each White student and $19.51 for each African American student in 1948.[i] But Marshall argued that even if the same was spent on Black students as on White ones, segregation was *inherently* damaging to African Americans. Citing research including studies by psychologists Kenneth and Mamie Clark, Marshall argued that segregation caused self-hatred in African American students. He also suggested that the roots of segregation lay in White supremacists' determination to hold African Americans back.

In the decision, the Supreme Court stated that educational facilities segregated by race were *inherently* unequal and therefore violated the Fourteenth Amendment. Marshall had achieved a historic advance for African Americans.

This was the heyday of the civil rights movement, but it was also the time of McCarthyism, with its hunt for Communist agents everywhere. This hurt many African Americans on the political Left, as well as the trade union movement. For instance, Paul Robeson's passport was revoked in 1950, and W.E.B. Du Bois was denied his passport in 1952. (He eventually moved to Ghana, where he stayed until his death.) Some of the most celebrated African American writers of the time were émigrés: Richard Wright lived in Paris, and James Baldwin also moved to France.

But these years would have a lasting impact on American life. Discrimination was outlawed, and the victories won by African Americans would help others fight discrimination based on their race, color, origin, or religion. Segregated public space was replaced by color-

---

[i] Franklin and Higginbotham, *From Slavery to Freedom*, 476.

blind public space, and America started to grow toward a diverse and equal society that recognized the dignity of all its citizens, including those of color.

Chapter 5: The Quest for Racial Equality in the 1960s and 1970s

Although discrimination had been outlawed and segregated schooling was on the way out, changes in attitudes and behavior were not so easy to accomplish. African Americans continued to suffer from prejudice in many areas of their lives, and many had grown tired of the "softly, softly" approach of the NAACP. They wanted more direct action.

Southern states, in particular, had lagged. In 1956, there were forty African Americans in state legislatures, but every one of them came from a Northern state. In the South, Jim Crow was still lurking around, and even federal enforcement agencies sometimes had a tough time getting past him.

The Montgomery Bus Boycott inspired several other approaches in which individuals worked collectively to challenge social attitudes. The Congress of Racial Equality (CORE) had been founded in 1942 as a non-violent organization that would use civil disobedience to challenge racism in the US. By the 1960s, it had chapters in most of the larger cities and an increasing number of chapters on college campuses. Youth would become a very important part of the civil rights movement in this era, for instance in Harlem, where CORE joined Columbia students in protests against the Vietnam War.

While buses and schools were now (in theory, at least) desegregated, private organizations still frequently maintained segregation. On February 1, 1960, four African American students sat down at a segregated lunch counter in a Woolworth five-and-dime in Greensboro, North Carolina. They were refused service, but they did not leave; they sat there until the store closed. They came back with other students the next day, and on the third day of the protests, more than sixty students turned up. The following day, more than 300 came, and the protest expanded to include the lunch counter at the S. H. Kress & Co. store.

Sales at the boycotted stores dropped by as much as a third. By July, Woolworth was suffering big losses. Management made the decision to desegregate the lunch counters in almost all its stores. Portions of the Greensboro lunch counter are now on display in the National Museum of American History in Washington, D.C., and in the Greensboro History Museum.

The Greensboro protest was covered by *The New York Times* and other national media. Sit-ins spread across the South. Though there had already been several sit-ins before Greensboro, the media coverage boosted the movement dramatically. There were sit-ins in Nashville, Charlotte, Tallahassee, Charleston, Tuskegee, Montgomery, Tampa, Daytona Beach, Little Rock, and New Orleans. Some students risked jail to make their point, like those from Friendship College in Rock Hill, South Carolina, who refused to pay bail when they were arrested at a lunch counter sit-in in 1961.

In Albany, Georgia, freedom songs first became part of the demonstrations. Spirituals such as "We Shall Overcome," "Keep Your Eyes on the Prize," "Let My People Go," and "Tree of Life" helped motivate and enhance the unity of the demonstrators.

CORE launched another style of action with its Freedom Rides in 1961, sending groups of volunteers through the South on bus trips to test whether transportation had been properly desegregated. In many cases, state governments and bus companies had simply ignored the Supreme Court rulings that mandated desegregated transport. The Freedom Riders moved in mixed racial groups, White and Black protestors together. The Student Nonviolent Coordinating Committee (SNCC) joined CORE in organizing these rides. While these were intended to be peaceful protests, the Ku Klux Klan (aided by the police) incited mob violence at the rides in Anniston and Birmingham, Alabama. In Anniston, the bus was set on fire, and the riders narrowly escaped lynching.

Many of the Freedom Riders were arrested. In fact, the rides were organized to get as many taken into jail as possible, attempting to block the jail system with hundreds of demonstrators. The rides spread to include sit-ins at segregated restaurants and hotels.

While some mainstream media portrayed the riders as disorderly and provocative, many people were inspired by the movement, particularly by the fact that Northerners were flocking to the Southern states to help Southern African Americans. The voter registration campaigns of the 1960s in many cases grew out of the Freedom Ride campaigns.

As seen in the violent response of the KKK and other White supremacists to the Freedom Rides, the White South did not intend to surrender quietly. African Americans who attempted to claim their rights faced obstructive or violent responses. For instance, in 1962, African American student James Meredith's attempt to register at the University of Mississippi in Oxford, Mississippi, had to be safeguarded by federal marshals. A riot killed two students before President Kennedy had to call on the National Guard to restore order.

Then, on June 11, 1963, George Wallace, the segregationist Governor of Alabama, stood at the door of the Foster Auditorium at the University of Alabama to block the entrance of two African American students in an incident known as the "Stand at the Schoolhouse Door." President Kennedy had to federalize the National Guard, as Eisenhower had done, against its own state governor. The Guard general asked Wallace to step aside, which he eventually did.

While President Kennedy appeared to be generally pro civil rights and had met with Dr. King as early as 1961, he did not take decisive action early on. Obstructive officials in the South were able to keep backtracking. A meeting between African American writer James Baldwin and the Kennedys ended in failure. Kennedy apparently did not really understand the issues. But at least the Kennedy administration decided to act, pushing for civil rights legislation.

Nonetheless, there was impatience among the African American community in 1963. Civil disobedience continued, and in April, a broad civil rights campaign that included both sit-ins and marches began in Birmingham, Alabama, disrupting the Easter shopping season and thereby attacking the structures of White economic power.

Within two weeks, an injunction was issued against demonstrations, boycotts, pickets, and parades. This was ignored by the leaders of the campaign. On Good Friday, the campaigners marched as planned. Martin Luther King Jr., Fred Shuttleworth of the Alabama Christian Movement for Human Rights, and SCLC's Ralph Abernathy were arrested, together with other marchers.

In Birmingham jail, Dr. King wrote his "Letter from Birmingham Jail," starting his work in the margins of a newspaper because he had no writing paper available. In response to accusations that the campaign was led by "outsiders," he said that "Injustice anywhere is a threat to justice everywhere ... Whatever affects one directly, affects all indirectly."[i]

Working for civil rights could be dangerous. Medgar Evers, the NAACP field secretary in Mississippi (and a man who had fought in the Normandy landings) was murdered in 1963. Byron De La Beckwith, a White supremacist and member of the KKK, was accused of the murder. He was tried twice in 1964, both times with an all-White jury that refused to convict. New evidence had come to light by 1994 when he was tried again and finally convicted. But, as is so often the case, it seemed that African Americans had to wait a long time for justice.

Medgar Evers.[i]

---

[i] Martin Luther King Jr., "Letter from a Birmingham Jail," University of Pennsylvania Africa Studies Center, Accessed April 2, 2025, https://www.africa.upenn.edu/Articles_Gen/Letter_Birmingham.html.

The year 1963 was not all pain. On August 28, a crowd of over 250,000 brought civil rights to the fore at the March on Washington. One man had roller-skated there from Chicago; the United Auto Workers' five-thousand-strong contingent was bussed in.

Asa Philip Randolph of the Brotherhood of Sleeping Car Porters organized the march to bring the labor movement and the civil rights movement together. Also prominent among the organizers were Roy Wilkins (president of the NAACP), John Lewis of the SNCC, Dr. King, Joachim Prinz of the American Jewish Congress, Mathew Ahmann of the National Catholic Conference for Interracial Justice, and other church and trades union leaders. Black and White leaders worked together to get Black and White people marching together.

But the day is remembered best for Martin Luther King Jr.'s celebrated speech, "I Have a Dream." While his "Letter from Birmingham Jail" justified the civil rights campaign and the use of civil disobedience, this speech gave African Americans a vision for the future and the optimism that they could achieve that future. It caught the mood of the day and remains an inspiration for many.

Yet the forces of reaction had not been beaten. Two weeks later, the 16th Street Baptist Church in Birmingham, Alabama, was bombed by the Ku Klux Klan, killing four young African American girls. Dr. King sent a telegram to segregationist governor George Wallace: "The blood of our little children is on your hands."[i] Two months after that, Kennedy was assassinated.

While Kennedy took some time to appreciate the urgency of federal action on civil rights, he had nonetheless appointed African Americans to high federal offices—judges, heads of departments, and presidential advisors. He had already envisaged a civil rights act making segregation in public facilities and discrimination in employment illegal. His promise was faithfully kept by his successor, Lyndon B. Johnson, who put the act through in 1964.

The summer of 1964 was Freedom Summer, in which numerous civil rights organizations sponsored a campaign to register African American voters in the state of Mississippi. The SNCC, Southern Christian Leadership Conference, CORE, and NAACP joined forces to bring

---

[i] "16th Street Baptist Church Bombing (1963)," National Park Service, accessed April 2, 2025, https://www.nps.gov/articles/16thstreetbaptist.htm.

bright students from northern and western universities into the project. Ninety percent were White, and a large number were Jewish.

Mississippi was chosen because, in 1962, only 6.2 percent of Black voters in Mississippi were registered, the lowest percentage in any state. Prospective voters had to demonstrate their knowledge of the 285-section state constitution to the (White) registrars, who debarred many Black voters. In any case, the extended quizzing must have deterred many from applying to vote in the first place.

Freedom Summer wasn't just about increasing the number of Black registered voters, though; it was about legally challenging the basis of that low registration, setting up local support services, getting coverage by the national press, and establishing "Freedom Schools"—summer schools that taught constitutional rights, Black history, and how to run a political campaign, as well as helping improve math ability and literacy rates. Freedom libraries were also established in many towns.

This may sound like a cute way for entitled White kids to spend the summer vacation. But civil rights workers helping to register African American voters in Mississippi risked their lives. Violence against activists was common, and three volunteers were murdered by Klansmen.

But Freedom Summer did not fail. It tripled the number of Black voters in Mississippi, and for the first time, it focused national attention on the plight of African American voters in the Southern states. Perhaps as a result, White politicians used less and less race-baiting in their speeches. Many younger people became politicized during these events. On the other hand, some Black activists felt that Freedom Summer had, indeed, been a bit too White and moved closer to a Black Power approach to future events.

It's worth noticing that Freedom Summer's historical importance was not limited to 1964 or to Mississippi. Marshall Ganz, one of the field workers in Freedom Summer, learned his political organizing smarts in Mississippi, and in 2008, he played a crucial role in organizing Barack Obama's election campaign.

In 1964, Martin Luther King Jr. won the Nobel Peace Prize.

This was a time when other ethnicities were also fighting for freedom. For instance, El Movimiento, the Chicano Movement, aimed to reclaim the term "Chicano," a racial insult, as a badge of pride in defiance of White Anglo-Saxon Protestant (WASP) norms. Units such as the Brown

Berets and the Mexican American Youth Organization (MAYO) fought prejudice against Hispanics. Many of their struggles were like those of the NAACP, such as segregated schooling. *Mendez v. Westminster* (1947) won a ruling that segregating children of Latin descent was unconstitutional. These common experiences of segregation and racism led to a movement of Black-Brown unity.

At the same time, Native Americans were fighting for recognition. For instance, they were struggling against their children being sent to boarding schools to be "educated out of" being Native. They were in many cases unable to govern their own communities effectively and did not own their tribal lands or had been compelled to lease them out. The American Indian Movement, founded in 1968, drew much of its inspiration from the NAACP and the leaders of the civil rights movement.

Another area of liberation during the 1970s and 1980s was sexual liberation. Feminism, rather than simply seeking equal opportunities for women, started to critique the patriarchal system and the way society was organized in response to male needs and desires. French writer Simone de Beauvoir had shown how women are seen as "other" by a male-dominated society, with the male always considered the norm. In 1963, Betty Friedan's *The Feminine Mystique* showed how women whose lives were limited to their nuclear family often showed signs of sadness and even depression. The happy nuclear family shown in advertisements, she averred, was a myth.

The foundation of the National Organization for Women (NOW) in 1966 gave women a significant voice in national politics. At the same time, the availability of the contraceptive pill from 1961 onward put women in control of their own bodies and destinies.

The concept of intersectionality was also developed during the late 1960s. According to this concept, all groups that are marginalized by mainstream society share common interests, as all types and forms of discrimination combine and overlap. However, many Black women felt that feminism was biased toward the experience and needs of middle- and upper-class White women and overlooked the particular challenges of Black women's "double handicap." Black

The gay liberation movement kicked off with the Stonewall riots in Manhattan in June 1969 when a crowd in Greenwich Village fought back against a police raid of the Stonewall Inn, a bar that welcomed gay customers. The movement echoed other liberation movements, using the "Gay Power" slogan (echoing Black Power). Huey Newton of the Black Panthers supported both women's liberation and gay liberation, refusing to see African Americans as the only people discriminated against.

The various liberation movements also created new academic fields, with women's studies and Black history arriving on the syllabus. San Diego State University was the first to establish a women's studies program, while San Francisco State had already created a Black studies department in 1968. White male society had overlooked the contributions of women and African Americans to history and literature. It was the task of these departments to reevaluate culture and history in the light of these overlooked perspectives.

Black separatism had always bubbled under the surface of the civil rights movement, but now there was a new sense of urgency. The two main parties no longer represented many of the views of African Americans, and there was a desire to move away from them and create a new political force.

Stokely Carmichael, one of the Freedom Riders and leader of the SNCC, started to speak about Black Power. He rejected assimilation into the White middle class, which he saw as validating the dominant culture. Black people needed to make their own politics and society outside the White power structure and its institutions. He did not advocate separatism as such but believed Black people should deal with White people from a position of economic, cultural, and psychological self-sufficiency. (This is not unlike Booker T. Washington's assertion that African Americans needed to gain economic self-sufficiency before they could win social equality.)

Eventually, he left the United States for Africa with his wife Miriam Makeba, a Black South African singer. In Guinea, he became known as Kwame Ture and worked with the All-African People's Revolutionary Party.

One of Carmichael's key contributions to thought was the idea of institutional racism—the way in which an institution such as the police, a university, or a political party can embody racism within its organization, thus failing to provide a service to people of color.

The Black Panther Party brought Marxism to the struggle for Black Power. Founded by Huey Newton and Bobby Seale in 1966, it saw the fight for African Americans' rights as part of the international class struggle. It also aimed to focus the discontent and anger of Black youth. Although social issues such as the Free Breakfast for School Children Program took up much of the Black Panthers' time, they gained a reputation for violence. In particular, they carried guns (legally) when observing police patrols of Black neighborhoods.

A key Black Panther demand was for a United Nations plebiscite to allow African Americans to decide their own destiny. They defined Black Americans as a colonized and exploited people and quoted from anti-colonialist authors like Che Guevara, Frantz Fanon, and Ho Chi Minh. (However, their language was gendered, tending to exclude Black women. Eldridge Cleaver, a leader of the Panthers, claimed that Black women were silent allies of White men and that Black men needed to control them to gain respect.)

The Black Panthers helped inspire a generation of new African American activists, though the Black Power movement was never monolithic. The movement was brought together by its symbols: the raised fist, the Afro hair style, and the red, black, and green African colors (sometimes united in the pan-African Marcus Garvey flag).

For African American women, "going natural" with their hair instead of using straighteners and relaxers to try to copy White hairstyles was a major political statement, a rejection of assimilation. "Black is beautiful" challenged the White view of Black bodies as unlovely, asserting the value of natural African hair and darker skin tones.

The Nation of Islam (NOI) became prominent during the 1960s and 1970s. Originally founded in 1930 and led by Elijah Muhammad (Elijah Poole) from 1934, the NOI started to attract high-profile members such as Muhammad Ali (Cassius Clay Jr.) the boxer and Black separatist Malcolm X. NOI members see Christianity as one of the tools used by White supremacists to maintain their control of society. Islam offers them an alternative, authentically Black identity. (However, most mainstream Muslims do not see NOI as a truly Islamic movement.)

Malcolm X joined the Nation of Islam while in prison. (He eventually split from NOI, which was implicated in his assassination in 1965.) He had rejected non-violence, pointing out that White supremacists had never committed to non-violent action. His parents had been followers of Marcus Garvey, and like them, he believed that African Americans must be responsible for their own salvation. Until they took up that burden, he believed they were still effectively enslaved.

Malcolm X was portrayed in the mainstream press as a fire-breathing revolutionary who hated White people. In reality, he was a thoughtful man whose message evolved over time. He started as a petty criminal and ended as a devout and charismatic preacher. Like many Black Power leaders, his discourse was about manliness and masculinity. He belittled the civil rights leadership as cowards unwilling to fight for their freedom. He also linked the struggle with anticolonial movements across the world, making trips to the Middle East and Africa, and seeing African Americans as victims of colonialization just like peoples of the global South.

Sister Mary Roger Thibodeaux was a Roman Catholic nun who espoused the struggle for racial justice. Her 1972 book *A Black Nun Looks at Black Power* stressed that liberation was a holy cause: "Black Power is not foreign to Yahweh and Yahweh is not foreign to Black Power. There is a covenant of friendship there. The cause of Justice is and always will be in strict accordance with the Will of God."[i]

The link with anticolonialism was a strong one. Writer Richard Wright, then living in Paris, had attended the 1955 Bandung Conference of Asian and African peoples. He knew Kwame Nkrumah, the future prime minister of Ghana, to which Wright had traveled. "This meeting of the rejected was in itself a kind of judgment upon the western world," he wrote, counting both Africans and Black Americans among the "rejected."[ii]

Meanwhile, the civil rights movement continued its agenda of legal test cases and peaceful demonstrations. However, the police did not always keep these demonstrations peaceful. For instance, on Bloody Sunday, March 7, 1965, state police attacked a march from Selma to Montgomery, Alabama. Ironically, the march was being held to protest police brutality—specifically, the fatal shooting of activist Jimmie Lee Jackson during a demonstration.

The march was led by John Lewis of the SNCC (later a member of the House of Representatives and dean of the Georgian congressional

---

[i] Mary Roger Thibodeaux, *A Black Nun Looks at Black Power* (Sheed & Ward, 1972).

[ii] Richard Wright. *Black Power: Three Books from Exile: Black Power; The Color Curtain; and White Man, Listen!* (Harper Collins, 2008).

delegation) and Rev. Hosea Williams of the SCLC. The marchers' way across the Edmund Pettus Bridge was blocked by state police, who then attacked the activists. Two days later, the White Unitarian minister Rev. James Reeb, a member of the SCLC who had gone to Selma to join the march, was beaten to death by White supremacists.

News reports that showed peaceful Black students attacked by angry White people resulted in a national outcry. Media attention also foregrounded the fact that many Black Southerners still had no effective vote. The third march, starting March 21, was protected by the full might of the state, President Johnson having federalized the Alabama National Guard to ensure the safe passage of the demonstrators.

The president then held a joint session of Congress to ask senators and representatives to pass legislation on voting rights. The 1965 Voting Rights Act outlawed racial discrimination in voting, making racially motivated gerrymandering, literacy tests, and other refusals to register qualified voters illegal. It also set up a system for federal examiners to ensure the voter registration process was correctly run (repealed in 2006).

Lyndon B. Johnson, addressing Congress, explicitly used the language of the civil rights movement. "It is not just Negroes but all of us who must overcome the crippling legacy of bigotry and injustice," he said. "And we shall overcome."[i]

The late '60s brought two historic firsts. In 1967, Thurgood Marshall, the NAACP's special counsel, became the first African American appointed to the Supreme Court, on which he would serve for nearly a quarter of a century. And, in 1968, the first interracial kiss on US network TV was shown between Captain James T. Kirk of the U.S.S. *Enterprise* and Lieutenant Nyota Uhura in *Star Trek*.

In 1968, however, tragedy struck. Dr. Martin Luther King Jr. was assassinated while standing on the balcony of his hotel in Memphis, Tennessee. His personal appeal, convincing oratory, and quiet dignity had greatly benefited the civil rights movement; he was now a martyr for the cause. There were riots following his death in many cities, and though James Earl Ray was soon charged with the murder, many

---

[i] Colleen Shogan, "'We Shall Overcome': Lyndon B. Johnson and the 1965 Voting Rights Act," The White House Historical Association, April 8, 2021. Whitehousehistory.org/we-shall-overcome-lbj-voting-rights.

suspected a conspiracy. Jesse Jackson believed the government had helped set up the assassination.

That same year, segregationist George Wallace ran as a third-party candidate for president. He managed to gain 13 percent of the popular vote and forty-six electoral college votes. Clearly, there were still plenty of people backing Jim Crow, though not enough to prevent Nixon's election.

While voting was the big issue in the South, in the Northern states, it was equal access to housing. The courts had upheld racially restrictive real estate covenants that denied African Americans equal access to housing, while the Federal Housing Administration's strategy of pursuing "stability" effectively entrenched both racial and class bias. Furthermore, banks' redlining—refusal to lend to Black Americans moving into "White" neighborhoods—meant that Black owner/occupiers had restricted choice of property.

Yet, by the end of the 1970s, a Black middle class was forming. It seemed that the American Dream was at last accessible to African Americans. Federal authorities had finally tired of segregationists' reluctance to implement equalities laws. The Supreme Court (now, of course, including Thurgood Marshall) ruled in *Alexander v. Holmes County Board of Education* (1969) that integration must be immediately implemented. *Brown* had ruled that it should occur "with all deliberate speed," but nearly fifteen years later, the Supreme Court concluded that the job needed to be finished. There was to be no more wiggle room.

In 1977, Alex Haley's miniseries *Roots* aired on ABC, a drama that told the story of an African American family—a Mandinka boy growing up in Africa, going through slavery and the civil war, and eventually gaining freedom. It became a phenomenon, with 130 million Americans watching the broadcasts, and was followed by a sequel, *Roots: The Next Generations*, in 1979.

The 1980s brought African Americans up-to-date with the new Black middle class in the form of the Huxtable family in *The Cosby Show*. This sitcom was a huge success, becoming the number one rated show for five successive seasons, and it opened the way for more shows to feature African American majority casts.

Black women also, at last, came into prominence with a new generation of writers: Toni Morrison, Alice Walker, Audre Lorde, and Maya Angelou. Autobiography was important to them as a way of addressing views about gender, race, and sexuality. For instance, Angelou's *I Know Why the Caged Bird Sings* (1969) recounts her rape by her mother's boyfriend and analyzes the struggle of a Black girl to find her identity.

Feminism, though, was racially problematic. Alice Walker coined the word "womanist" since she found that mainstream feminism was overly concentrated on White women's goals. Black women started to create their own forums, such as the Third World Women's Alliance and the National Black Feminist Association.

In the 1980s, Jesse Jackson campaigned twice for the Democratic Party presidential nomination. He won 24 percent of the votes in primaries in 1988, losing to Michael Dukakis. George Bush won the presidential election, but Dukakis took 90 percent of African Americans' votes. During Bush's government, African Americans achieved high offices. Colin Powell became chairman of the Joint Chiefs of Staff, Edward J. Perkins was director general of the Foreign Service (later, under Clinton, he was made ambassador to Australia), and Condoleezza Rice became secretary of state.

Chapter 6: The Rise of the Black Entrepreneur

One thing that's not much appreciated about Black entrepreneurs is that they have always been there—right from the beginning of the modern history of North America. Jean-Baptiste Pointe du Sable (probably Haitian, though he may have been a French Canadian) set up a trading settlement in 1779. Later, he operated a ferry across the Missouri in St. Charles. He's now regarded as the founder of Chicago, of which his trading settlement was the original hub.

At the start of the 1840s California Gold Rush, Black entrepreneurs thrived—though some White gold diggers brought Black slaves with them. Free Black Americans headed west for the gold fields. Reuben Ruby made $600 in a month (the equivalent of $24,200 today). Others ran businesses such as general stores and freight haulage. Later, though, the White majority started to take over these businesses, limiting the opportunities for Black businesses. Many decided to head north to the goldfields of British Columbia, which had a major advantage over California: no Fugitive Slave Act.

Other free Black Americans ran craft businesses. For instance, James Forten served his apprenticeship as a sailmaker in Philadelphia and eventually bought the sail loft from his boss. He developed new equipment to make the job more efficient and created a highly profitable business, employing Black and White workers alike and becoming one of the wealthiest men in Philadelphia. He also supported abolitionist causes and civil rights and helped fund the startup of *The Liberator* newspaper in 1831. Captain Absalom Boston of Nantucket (who, as you may remember, had his own whaling ship) ran an inn. He, too, helped abolitionist causes and fought for civil rights for African Americans.

James Forten[5]

Even in the South, some African Americans managed to make their way in business. Elizabeth Keckley was born enslaved to the man who had fathered her and was brutally treated, but she used her skill with the sewing needle to her advantage. The family that owned her was supported by her earnings as a seamstress, but eventually she secured a loan from one of her customers to buy freedom for herself and her son. In 1860, she moved to Washington, D.C., where she set up as a dressmaker, becoming a top fashion trendsetter and employing a staff of twenty. She made clothes for the wives of eminent politicians, including Mary Todd Lincoln; she was even sometimes asked to help tame the president's hairstyle. It was she who introduced Sojourner Truth to Lincoln.

Elizabeth Keckley.[6]

Many slaves had excellent skill sets, as slave owners focused on training them in areas that would make money for themselves. Blacksmiths and dressmakers could be leased out, but it was difficult for new businesses to find credit. Elizabeth Keckley's dependence on financial support from her customers was a typical way of securing funds.

During Reconstruction and afterward, Black businesses in the South started to flourish. In some ways, Jim Crow laws actually helped Black businessmen since small businesses could serve the Black community—and White businesses often had no interest in Black customers. W.E.B. Du Bois and Booker T. Washington both urged Black Americans to become entrepreneurs, achieving economic independence and freeing themselves from dependence on an employer. Booker T. Washington set up the National Negro Business League to help them do so. By 1907, there were Black business districts in Chicago, New York, and several other cities.

Madam C. J. Walker was the first child in her family to be born free, in 1867. She started off as a domestic servant and then a laundress but eventually started working for a major cosmetics firm. In 1905, she took the knowledge she had acquired and founded her own company, focusing on products for African American women, such as hair straighteners. Hers was the first beauty products company to use uniformed sales agents to make house calls. She became a millionaire but also enriched many other African American women, who were able to build businesses as "Walker Agents." Her sales force numbered over 5,000 women nationwide.

Like many other Black businesspeople, Madam C. J. Walker put her wealth at the service of the African American community, supporting the NAACP and using her home in New York as a center for bringing Black leaders together. Her daughter, A'Lelia, took over the business and became a major patron of the Harlem Renaissance and African American musicians.

Maggie Lena Walker (no relation) created the St. Luke Penny Savings Bank, with a strong female customer base. Many washerwomen put their savings in this bank, which grew out of a mutual aid society in Richmond, Virginia. Many Black businesses, like this one, grew out of African American self-help initiatives (for instance, in insurance—often a problem for Black households).

In Tulsa, Oklahoma, so many Black businesses flourished in the Greenwood District that it was known as "Black Wall Street." African American professionals such as attorneys, doctors, and realtors (as well as hotels, barbershops, and general stores) catered to an all-Black clientele.

In fact, Greenwood was the advent of Black developers. J. B. Stradford bought up tracts of land in Tulsa from 1899 onward and built the Stradford Hotel. O.W. Gurley moved from Arkansas to Tulsa in 1906 and bought forty acres of land which he sold "only to colored," starting a rooming house and an African American Masonic lodge. Both these men believed that African Americans needed to work together and support each other.

However, as Greenwood became more and more successful, the inhabitants and businesses in nearby White suburbs began to feel threatened. When, in 1921, a Black shoe shiner was accused of assaulting a White woman, these low-level tensions exploded into violence. In the Tulsa Race Massacre, up to 300 African Americans were killed, and the entire area was looted and burned. (The official record showed only thirty-six deaths.) Ten thousand African Americans had been rendered homeless, and the city refused to compensate them.

In addition to entrepreneurs, many African American inventors built their careers on the back of technical or scientific knowledge. Booker T. Washington's promotion of scientific and technical learning as a way for African Americans to become self-sufficient had given many the skills and knowledge they needed to innovate. One of them was George Washington Carver, who worked at Tuskegee Institute. He developed new vegetable varieties, including improved peanuts, new sweet potatoes, and "Carver's Hybrid" cotton, as well as new dyes, linoleum, and synthetic rubber and glues.

Andrew Jackson Beard was born enslaved and started free life as a farmer. However, he had a quick and active mind and a very practical nature. For instance, having worked in a flour mill, he decided that he could easily build one of his own. In 1881, he developed a new double plow that allowed the distance between the two plow plates to be adjusted; later, he improved that design by including pitch adjustment. In 1882, he patented a rotary engine, and from 1890 to 1892, he dramatically improved the railroad coupler. Previous designs had required railway men to drop a peg into the coupler as the wagons were rolled together—a dangerous proceeding. His design worked automatically and was soon made compulsory. (The railroad coupler invention grew out of his own personal experience. Beard had lost a leg while attempting to couple two wagons. You could say that he had "skin in the game.")

Other railroad-based inventions by African Americans included Elijah McCoy's lubricator cup, which allowed machines to be oiled while in use rather than having to stop them for maintenance, and Granville T. Woods's invention of the third rail. Woods held more than fifty patents, successfully defending himself twice against Thomas Edison's claims of prior invention.

Garrett Augustus Morgan was also a prolific inventor, despite having attended school only to sixth grade. However, he hired a tutor while he was working and continued his studies privately. His first inventions were a zigzag attachment and a belt fastener for sewing machines. Later, he developed haircare products, including hair straightening cream, as well as the smoke hood (precursor of the gas mask) in 1912. A hero as well as an inventor, he used his own smoke hood to lead the rescue of several men from the Waterworks Tunnel in Cleveland, Ohio—in his pajamas! Modern life would not be the same without Morgan: he transformed the modern city with his patent for the traffic light (1925). His last invention never took off but was imaginative: a self-extinguishing cigarette.

African Americans are still inventing. Madison "Maddy" Maxey founded Loomia, a company that makes wearable electronics and e-textiles, in 2013, marrying her fashion sense to her love of technology. And there are now 161,031 firms with majority Black or African American ownership, up from 124,004 in 2017.[i] But that's still only 3 percent of total businesses in the US, compared to 13.6 percent of the population.

Several problems still face African American entrepreneurs. For instance, Black entrepreneurs get 40 percent less funding than White entrepreneurs, and they are denied funding twice as often, according to the Federal Reserve. When they do get funded, their finance may come with more onerous conditions attached. No wonder banks are not the first place they look for support! And since African American families generally have lower household wealth than White Americans, they have fewer assets to pledge as collateral or to use as seed capital.

There are currently about twenty Black-owned banks in the US. They tend to be smaller than White-owned banks, and few are nationwide. However, they have a mission to serve the Black community. OneUnited Bank in Boston, Los Angeles, and Miami; Harbor Bank of Maryland; Industrial Bank of Washington, D.C.; Citizens Trust Bank of Atlanta; and Carver Federal Savings Bank of New York City are five of the biggest. They don't just help by lending to Black individuals and businesses; they also help improve financial literacy in the Black community.

There are also signs of change following the Black Lives Matter protests. Major banks such as Citi and JP Morgan Chase have set aside millions of dollars for funding African American and Latinx businesses,

---

[i] "Census Bureau Releases New Data on Minority-Owned, Veteran-Owned, and Women-Owned Businesses," United States Census Bureau, October 26, 2023.
https://www.census.gov/newsroom/press-releases/2023/annual-business-survey-employer-business-characteristics.html.

and Citi has entered partnerships with sixteen Black-owned banks to provide targeted lending to both residential and commercial sectors, investing a total $100 million. Most Black entrepreneurs still look to the Black community for funding and assistance.

Black businesspeople have generally supported the civil rights movement. In fact, smaller Black businesses were often directly involved. For instance, pharmacist Richard Harris ran a carpool hub from his store to provide transport for African Americans during the Montgomery bus boycott, and gas station owner Amzie Moore helped with the logistics for Freedom Summer.

Ever since Booker T. Washington, the African American community has helped set up organizations to support Black training and entrepreneurship. Today's start-ups benefit from many such organizations, for instance the National Black MBA Association, Harlem Capital, U.S. Black Chambers, Inc., African Business Roundtable, and the Black Business and Professional Association. The #BankBlack movement is based on the idea of recirculating money within the community and has led to some $60 million moving to Black-owned banks and credit unions, where it can be lent to African American homeowners and Black-owned businesses.

Despite these handicaps, African American business has made great strides since the 1970s. In 1971, haircare company Johnson Products Company, noted for its "Afro Sheen," was the first Black-owned business to head for the American Stock Exchange. (It was later bought by Procter & Gamble.) It took until 1999 for the first Black CEO to be appointed at a Fortune 500 company—Franklin D. Raines, who came to Fannie Mae from the Clinton administration.

In 2003, Oprah Winfrey became the first African American billionaire. Her journey from childhood deprivation to wealth and influence is a potent inspiration for others, and she has used her position to promote Black businesses. For instance, in 2023, her "Favorite Things" list included products from thirty-two Black-owned businesses.

While Oprah is best known as a TV presenter, she is also a major business figure as CEO of Harpo Productions, which was responsible for the production of *The Oprah Winfrey Show*, as well as its network deals and magazines. Subsidiary Harpo Films produced films of particular interest to an African American audience, including *Beloved* (1998) based on the Toni Morrison novel, *Precious: Based on the Novel Push* by *Sapphire* (2009), *Selma* (2014) about the Selma, Montgomery, marches, and *The Color Purple* (2023) based on Alice Walker's novel.

Robert F. Smith of Vista Equity Partners is another African American billionaire who specializes in technology investment and is a major philanthropist. According to *Forbes*, he is the seventy-eighth richest person in the US and one of just fifteen Black billionaires worldwide. When he gave the commencement address at historically Black Morehouse College, he announced that he would pay the student loan debt of the entire graduating class. He also sponsored the college education of Nigerian girls who had been kidnapped by Boko Haram. He funds scholarships through the United Negro College Fund and has partnered with fintech firm Goalsetter to help a million Black and Latinx youth become shareholders.

African Americans remain underrepresented in the C-suite, and many Black businesses remain small, particularly in non-scalable sectors like service. However, many tech and finance companies are now actively pursuing diversity. For instance, Goldman Sachs operates a firmwide Black network in addition to a women's, Asian, disabled, and LGBTQ+ network and tries to ensure diversity among its supplier networks. When African Americans can rise to the top of their professions, they can help other Black businesses get started, so the effect can be far more important than a few internal promotions.

Black creativity and innovation have helped to shape America and, indeed, the modern world. And though there's further to go, the record so far shows that African Americans are definitely equal to the task.

Chapter 7: Women Who Shaped History

African American women had it hard from the very beginning. While the experience of slavery was traumatic for all enslaved people, it was particularly so for women. As we mentioned earlier, sexual violence was often employed as a tool for control or simply seen as a privilege of the master or overseer.

Many enslaved women bore children as a result of rape or relationships with an owner or a member of their owner's family, and they were denied a proper family life since their children represented a source of capital for the owner and might be sold away at any time. Worse, many would see their daughters go through the same experience of sexual violence. Many enslaved women who were in relationships with enslaved men saw their husbands and the fathers of their children sold away, leaving them responsible for their children's upbringing as single mothers. Women were often beaten in front of their male relatives, making the enslaved woman's body a site of shame and a pawn in an interracial masculine conflict.

Even after emancipation, African American women suffered from a double handicap. As African Americans, they were excluded from much of public life, and as women, they were given no vote and no voice. They were thus doubly discriminated against. But as Margaret Sloan, editor of

Ms. magazine, declared, "There can't be liberation for half a race."[i] Civil rights advances for African Americans that didn't include advances for Black women were, in her view, completely inadequate.

Back as early as the 1850s, Sojourner Truth had pointed out that Black power did not necessarily hand power to Black women. "There is a great stir about colored men getting their rights," she said, "but not a word about the colored women, and if colored men get their rights and colored women not theirs, the colored men will be masters over the women, and it will be just as bad as it was before."[ii]

When second wave feminism got going in the 1960s, it was led mainly by White middle-class women. Many Black women felt feminism was blind to their needs and even to their very existence. Instead, they adopted womanism—Alice Walker's word—which reconciles the empowerment of women with Black cultural values rather than taking the color-blind approach of mainstream feminism.

Sojourner Truth campaigned for abolition, but she was also an early womanist. Her speech "Ain't I a Woman?" drew on her own life experience to show women's strength, endurance, and thus eligibility for the vote: "I have borne thirteen children, and seen most all sold off to slavery, and when I cried out with my mother's grief, none but Jesus heard me! And ain't I a woman?" The speech also shows the lack of respect accorded to African American women: "That man over there says that women need to be helped into carriages, and lifted over ditches, and to have the best place everywhere. Nobody helps me any best place. And ain't I a woman?"[iii]

Born a slave, Sojourner experienced slavery at its worst. Brought up speaking Dutch on the Hardenbergh estate in New York, she was sold at nine to an English master who beat her, then again to a man who repeatedly raped her. Her love for an enslaved man on a neighboring farm was banned, as the man's owner would not own the children and so

---

[i] Barbara Campbell, "Black Feminists Form Group Here; National Body Hopes to End 'Myths' and Intimidation," *The New York Times*, August 16, 1973, https://www.census.gov/newsroom/press-releases/2023/annual-business-survey-employer-business-characteristics.html.

[ii] Franklin and Higgenbotham, *From Slavery to Freedom*, 243.

[iii] "Sojourner Truth: 'Ain't I a Woman?'" National Park Service, Accessed April 2, 2025, https://www.nps.gov/articles/sojourner-truth.htm.

received no advantage from it. She eventually married an older man and bore five children—one the result of rape by her master. Eventually, she ran away with her daughter, but her five-year-old son was illegally sold in Alabama. She had to take legal action to bring him home.

In 1843, she had a religious experience and changed her name from Isabella Baumfree to Sojourner Truth. She began an itinerant life, preaching the evils of slavery and advocating abolition. She spoke at abolitionist rallies and at suffragist conventions, sometimes singing a song or spiritual rather than making an oration.

She was not just a spiritual woman but a practical one. During the Civil War, she helped recruit Black troops for the Union Army and was invited to the White House by President Lincoln. (Later, President Grant also invited her.) She raised donations of food and clothing for the Black regiments and, after the war, tried to secure the grant of "forty acres and a mule" to former enslaved people.

Sojourner Truth with Abraham Lincoln.[7]

Like Sojourner Truth, Harriet Tubman made a huge contribution to the cause of abolition and helped promote women's suffrage. Also like Sojourner Truth, she was devoutly religious, and it was her religious beliefs that motivated her to act as she did. She was also born into slavery.

In 1849, Harriet escaped, finally reaching freedom in Philadelphia. She went back to rescue the rest of her family—first her niece Kessiah, then her younger brother Moses. However, when she tried to rescue her husband, she found he had married again and wanted to stay where he was. Instead, she rescued several other slaves. After this, she began her career as a "conductor" on the Underground Railroad, making fourteen more trips into the South at immense personal risk and freeing more than seventy enslaved people. Between trips, she worked as a domestic servant to get the funds for her mission.

Later, speaking of these years, she said: "I was conductor of the Underground Railroad for eight years, and I can say what most conductors can't say—I never ran my train off the track and I never lost a passenger."[1]

During the Civil War, Tubman helped refugees who had fled slavery in the South and served as a nurse in Port Royal. Later, she put her Underground Railroad experience of disguise, subterfuge, and secret travel to use and ran a scout group to reconnoiter for Union forces. Her intelligence was crucial to the taking of Jacksonville, Florida, and in the raid at Combahee Ferry. At Combahee Ferry, she also forewarned enslaved people, who came running for the boats when they heard the steamboats' whistles. More than 750 managed to escape.

Ida B. Wells is another African American woman who deserves to be better known. She was a groundbreaking female journalist and newspaper owner involved in both the crusade for civil rights (as a cofounder of the NAACP) and the movement for women's equality. Born into slavery, she found work in Memphis to support her younger siblings, first as a teacher, then as a reporter for the *Memphis Free Speech and Headlight.*

---

[1] Catherine Clinton, *Harriet Tubman: the Road to Freedom* (New York, 2004), 192.

She was also a predecessor of Rosa Parks, twice refusing to give up her seat in the ladies' car of the railway. Physically dragged out of the car by a conductor, she sued the railroad and won her case—but then lost on appeal.

In 1892, after a friend of hers was lynched, Ida started a crusade against racial violence, using investigative journalism as a tool to expose the savagery of the conditions under which Southern African Americans lived. In one piece she wrote: In 1892, after a friend of hers was lynched, Ida started a crusade against racial violence, using investigative journalism as a tool to expose the savagery of the conditions under which Southern African Americans lived. In one piece she wrote: "Twenty-eight human beings burned at the stake, one of them a woman and two of them children, is the awful indictment against American civilization—the gruesome tribute which the nation pays to the color line."[i]

After a White mob destroyed her newspaper offices in Memphis, Wells moved to New York, continuing her campaign against lynching with a pamphlet, *Southern Horrors: Lynch Law in All Its Phases*. She asserted that racial violence was White people's response to Black people's economic success, which they perceived as a threat. Most Americans in the Northern states had not, until then, realized the full extent of violence against Black people in the South. Extending her campaign, she toured Britain, reaching a wider audience, and worked for *The Daily Inter-Ocean*. She was the first African American woman to work as a journalist for a White-owned newspaper.

She also began writing for *The Chicago Conservator* and eventually married its founder, Ferdinand Lee Barnett, who was likewise involved in civil rights activism. She took over as editor of the paper, working with her husband in a truly equal partnership that was highly unusual at the time.

Her career is also interesting for the controversy she caused since, as a woman and suffragist, she upset many of the more conservative civil rights leaders. As a Black woman campaigning for civil rights, she often encountered a lack of understanding or even outright racism from White campaigners for the female vote. It illustrates well the way in which Black women belonged neither to the mainstream civil rights campaign nor to mainstream feminism—a problem that became evident in the 1960s.

---

[i] Please insert the source information for Ida's quote here.

Compared to these heroines of the struggle for civil rights, Josephine Baker at first sight looks rather frivolous. Some civil rights leaders found her presence at the March on Washington in 1963 inexplicable. She was a singer and dancer who, like many African Americans of her time, found Paris more welcoming to Black people than the America of her day. At the Folies Bergère, she was famed for her almost-nude act in which she wore a grass skirt decorated with bananas.

However, she was a woman of principle. She had always refused to perform for segregated audiences. During the Second World War, she became a member of the French Resistance, using her prominence as an entertainer to gather information from senior German officers who socialized in the night clubs of Paris. Later, she entertained free French troops in North Africa, organizing her own show and paying her own costs. As a result of her work for the French Resistance, she was awarded the Resistance Medal and the Croix de Guerre and made a member of the Légion d'honneur. In 2021, she was honored with a memorial in the French Panthéon, the first Black woman to be so honored.

Even though she had become a French citizen, she continued to support the civil rights movement in America. She spoke at the March on Washington, forthrightly referring to her experience of racism in the US. "I have walked into the palaces of kings and queens, and into the houses of presidents and much more. But I could not walk into a hotel in America and get a cup of coffee, and that made me mad. And when I get mad, you know that I open my big mouth. And then look out, 'cause when Josephine opens her mouth, they hear it all over the world."[i]

---

[i] "(1963) Josephine Baker, 'Speech at the March on Washington,'"BlackPast.org, Accessed April 2, 2025, https://web.archive.org/web/20180920010915/http://www.blackpast.org/1963-josephine-baker-speech-march-washington.

Josephine Baker in her banana costume.[8]

Mary McLeod Bethune was the daughter of former slaves who had bought their own land. She grew up picking cotton but benefited from the post-Civil War emphasis on educating African Americans, graduating from Scotia Seminary and then becoming a teacher herself. She was active in both civil rights and women's causes, becoming president of the National Association of Colored Women's Clubs in 1924, founding president of the National Council of Negro Women in 1935, and vice-president of the NAACP in 1940.

But when Mary founded her school for girls in Daytona, Florida, it was next to the town dump, and she had to finance it by selling sweet potato pies. She even got the builders to work for free by offering them tuition in return for their labor. Her school eventually became a full college and the kernel of Bethune-Cookman University. She also opened a hospital for African Americans—like the school, starting from scratch with just two beds, though soon holding twenty—and made the school library accessible to the whole community.

Bethune was a close friend of First Lady Eleanor Roosevelt and helped the Roosevelts form the Black Cabinet (the Federal Council of Negro Affairs), of which she was the only female member. Franklin D. Roosevelt also appointed her as head of the Division of Negro Affairs in the National Youth Administration, part of his New Deal. This made her the first African American to head a government agency.

She believed that African Americans—and White Americans, too—needed to be taught about the Black contribution to history. "If our people are to fight their way up out of bondage," she wrote, "we must arm them with the sword and the shield and the buckler of pride."[i]

While the 1950s civil rights movement is perhaps best known for the leadership of Martin Luther King Jr. and John Lewis, women played a huge part in the struggle. Rosa Parks's protest was the catalyst for the Montgomery bus boycott, while Coretta Scott King took up her husband's cause after his assassination and became a major force in her own right. Diane Nash led the Nashville sit-ins and supported the Freedom Riders after CORE withdrew. She was nominated for an NAACP award by Martin Luther King Jr.

---

[i] Mary McLeod Bethune, "Clarifying Our Vision with the Facts," *Journal of Negro History* 23, no. 1 (1938): 10-15, https://doi.org/10.2307/2714703.

Even in the "Big Six" of civil rights leaders, there was a woman: Dorothy Height. However, her contribution was often overlooked by the press. She was one of the organizers of the March on Washington, but she did not speak at it. She was president of the National Council of Negro Women from 1958 to 1990 and organized Wednesdays in Mississippi to bring together women of different races in the combat against segregation. Later in life, Dorothy became known for her eclectic collection of hats—many made by Black milliner Vanilla Beane. But she should be remembered for much more than that!

Some women found the civil rights movement limiting, with its expectation that women would serve mainly in supporting roles. Gloria Richardson also found non-violence a limitation, joining the more militant wing of the civil rights movement.

At Howard University, she was involved in protests at Peoples Drug, which would not hire Black workers, then at a segregated Woolworth lunch counter. When she moved back to Cambridge, Maryland, she got involved in civil rights, setting new goals for the movement: not just desegregation but fully equal access to housing, health care, and education. Eventually, she became the leader of the Cambridge Movement.

Some civil rights leaders saw her as "too confrontational." Often, male leaders who expected women to stay in the background were her main critics. She attracted particular criticism for opposing a city-wide referendum on segregation in Cambridge, but she was right to oppose White citizens being able to vote against Black rights in a citywide referendum. "A first-class citizen does not beg for freedom," she said. "A first-class citizen does not plead to the White power structure to give him something that the Whites have no power to give or take away. Human rights are human rights, not White rights."[i]

Gloria Richardson continued to be involved in the civil rights movement all her life; even in her nineties, she supported the Black Lives Matter protests.

Kathleen Cleaver was another "outlier," the only woman to serve on the top tier of the Black Panthers. She had learned how to organize

---

[i] Daniel Hardin, "Raging Civil Rights Struggle Leads to Union Victories: Cambridge MD 1938," Washington Area Spark, accessed April 2, 2025, https://washingtonareaspark.com/tag/gloria-richardson/.

activists in the SNCC, but when she married Eldridge Cleaver, she also took on the job of communications secretary for the Panthers. She organized the campaign to free Huey Newton. Later, when the Panthers split, she promoted the new party.

Kathleen spent time in Algeria and then North Korea, where her husband lived in exile after being charged with attempted murder after a confrontation between the Panthers and Oakland police officers. She was responsible for raising a defense fund and arranging his return to the US.

In the 1980s, she left Eldridge, who was shifting his politics to the Right and eventually became a conservative Republican. She went back to university and studied law, becoming involved in many legal and political campaigns, including the successful fight to overturn the death sentence on Mumia Abu-Jamal, a member of the Panthers. Another campaign helped overturn Panther Geronimo Ji-Jaga Pratt's murder conviction.

The difficulty of reconciling the movements for racial and gender equality can be clearly seen in the career of Aileen Hernandez. After attending Howard University, she started working in the trade union movement. Later, she was made the first female member of the Equal Employment Opportunity Commission. However, she felt obliged to resign because the commission would not address the issue of sexual harassment. As president of the National Organization for Women (NOW), she again felt compelled to resign when elections resulted in an all-White board for the second year in succession. She had already found NOW to be elitist and middle-class.

After these experiences, Hernandez cofounded Black Women Organized for Political Action. She was a pioneer of intersectionality, cofounding NOW's Minority Women's Task Force.

The civil rights era formed a whole new generation of African American women who believed there were no longer any limits on what they could achieve. One of these was Shirley Chisholm, who entered the House of Representatives in 1968 and ran a campaign for the Democratic Party presidential ticket in 1972 with the strapline "unbought and unbossed." Though unsuccessful in winning nomination, her sheer guts and brash honesty gave her the ability to open discussion on issues such as drugs, social justice, and the war in Vietnam.

Chisholm supported women's issues throughout her career, including supporting the 1970 Equal Rights Amendment. Initially, she hired only women for her office, at least half of them Black.

She noted, though, that she had suffered from the "double discrimination" against women of color throughout her career. On the other hand, she offered a new idea of American identity:

"I am not the candidate of Black America, although I am Black and proud. I am not the candidate of the women's movement of this country, although I am a woman and equally proud of that. I am the candidate of the people and my presence before you symbolizes a new era in American political history."[i]

During the 1970s and 1980s, Black women took on ever more prominence in the media and in politics. In 1975, Carole Simpson was the first Black woman to become a major network news anchor; she was later the first minority woman to moderate a presidential debate (Clinton v. Bush v. Ross Perot in 1992). Reynelda Muse and Norma Quarles anchored at CNN, and Charlayne Hunter-Gault joined the *MacNeil/Lehrer NewsHour* on PBS.

But the veteran of the new generation of Black broadcasters was Oprah Winfrey. She started out working in local radio and then TV in Nashville, Tennessee, and by the age of nineteen was co-anchoring the evening news. However, she was not fated to become a news journalist. Instead, she moved to Chicago to host a failing talk show, *AM Chicago*. In a few months, she took the show from the last to the first spot in the rankings; in 1986, the show signed a major syndication deal and was renamed *The Oprah Winfrey Show*.

Oprah brought a new empathy and emotional earthiness to the talk show, introducing subjects such as spirituality, mindfulness, personal growth, and self-development. She also brought a refreshing honesty about her own story, including being abused as a child and her weight problems. Through her show, she became incredibly influential, for instance with her book club, which could boost a book into the bestseller list overnight. She endorsed Barack Obama for the presidency in 2008 and backed Kamala Harris in 2024, hosting a virtual rally with Kamala in September.

---

[i] "Shirley Chisholm Addresses the National Women's Political Caucus," Harvard Radcliffe Institute, September 9, 2020. https://www.radcliffe.harvard.edu/news-and-ideas/shirley-chisholm-addresses-the-national-women-s-political-caucus.

Black women have also been prominent in the sciences. Katherine Johnson made the manned space missions of the 1960s possible. It was her calculations that set the trajectories, launch windows, and orbits for the spacecraft and plotted emergency return paths. Other African American women also worked within NASA's research division, culminating in the 1991 achievement of physician and engineer Mae C. Jemison, who became the first African American female astronaut.

But Black culture still sometimes holds women back. Hip-hop and rap music have come under fire for misogynistic lyrics and for commonly referring to women as "bitch" and "hoe" (whore). In some ways, the portrayal of Black women in rap music and videos harkens back to slavery-era stereotyping of African American women as sex objects.

In corporate America, stereotyping still keeps Black women out of leadership positions. Only 4 percent of C-suite executives are women of color.[i] So, there is still more work to do. Perhaps a female Black president could make a difference?

---

[i] Javacia Harris Bower, "How Executives Hold Back Black Women at Work," *Her Money*, May 30, 2024. https://hermoney.com/earn/careers/how-executives-hold-black-women-back-at-work/.

Chapter 8: The Evolution of Black Music

Black music is a testament to the resilience of African American culture. Immense creativity and emotional openness created music that changed the American soundscape. African Americans even created what has now become a typical American instrument: the banjo, a descendant of the gourd-bodied lutes and harps of Senegambia.

Sub-Saharan African musical traditions are very different from European classical music. They are characterized by polyrhythm (for instance playing a four-beat rhythm against a three-beat rhythm) and syncopation, moving the accent to what would normally be a downbeat. The melodies are often pentatonic, using just five notes in a scale—like playing only the black keys of a piano. Heterophony, in which different variants of a single melody are sung or played simultaneously, is also characteristic.

These musical traditions are also accompanied in most African cultures by dance, which may hold religious meaning. All these traditions were brought to America by enslaved Africans but developed differently in North America, South America, and the Caribbean.

One tradition that may have developed out of African music and dance is the "ring shout," in which Christian worshipers move in a circle while clapping and singing or praying. The "shout," or "praise break" is still a part of Pentecostal worship and has become part of modern gospel music, often used as an up-tempo finale to a song.

The "field holler," or "work song," used call and response, which became a part of later Black music styles such as gospel. Dances included jerking, shuffling, and hand-slapping, reflecting African dance styles rather than the stepping of European couple dances.

The Great Awakening in the 1740s and 1750s played a big part in African American culture. Revival meetings and Pentecostalism brought the influence of hymnody to African American music, but independent Black churches developed melismatic and expressive styles of singing that were quite different from the foursquare rhythms of White hymn singing. One was the practice of "deaconing," in which the elder would read two lines of a hymn, which were then repeated by the congregation.

"Spirichels" (spirituals) were recorded on Gullah Island. The African American spiritual evolved in the South and were potent expressions of yearning, grief, and longing, communicating the experience of slavery. Some were used as "code" songs to convey messages, for instance announcing meetings. "Signifyin'," expressing multiple or hidden meanings, was characteristic of spirituals and trickster stories alike, often conveying a coded meaning that could not be understood by White people.

Many spirituals use biblical episodes such as Moses freeing the Hebrew people as analogies for the longed-for emancipation of the enslaved. Originally oral traditions, spirituals began to be published after the Civil War, and ensembles like the Fisk Jubilee Singers started to tour with this material, popularizing the spiritual across America. (They are still touring today.)

Thomas A. Dorsey, the gospel music composer who wrote "Precious Lord," founded Dorsey House to publish African American music and ensure the profits were kept in the community. (Intriguingly, he had grown up in the blues scene as "Georgia Tom" before his religious conversion.)

However, African American musical traditions were often exploited by White singers. This was nothing new. Slaves who could sing or play music were often made to entertain their masters. "Blind Tom" Reene Wiggins, a piano virtuoso, earned $750,000 for his owners, who continued to exploit him even after the end of slavery.[i]

---

[i] Burton W. Peretti, *Lift Every Voice: The History of African American Music* (Rowman & Littlefield, 2009), 32.

A nastier piece of exploitation was the minstrel tradition, which played up to White nostalgia for the idealized Old South. White musicians would perform in blackface, portraying African Americans as dim-witted and lazy and featuring stereotypes such as the Black mammy, the dandy (Zip Coon), and the yaller girl, a provocative mulatto flirt (played by a man, like the other female characters). Thomas D. Rice's song "Jump Jim Crow" (1828) mimicked the dance of a lame stable hand: "Wheel about and turn about and do jus' so / Eb'ry time I wheel about I jump Jim Crow."

Jim Crow would, in time, give his name to the "Jim Crow" laws that enforced segregation.

But some African Americans also made money out of the minstrel shows; parodying yourself could pay well. In the late nineteenth century, Billy Kersands earned up to $100 a week as a comic blackface singer. He would fill his mouth with billiard balls to amuse the public. He was also an accomplished soft shoe dancer.

In the 1890s, ragtime started to become popular, with its lively syncopated rhythms. It brought the cakewalk, a dance that was influenced by the ring shout and involved stylized high stepping and strutting. This was the first time an African American dance had become popular in ballrooms.

The Black composer William Marion Cook had studied in Berlin and later with the composer Antonín Dvořák but found the classical music world highly segregated. He forsook it for the delights of musical theater. He conducted an all-White orchestra in his show *Clorindy, or The Origin of the Cake Walk* in 1898 and produced the musical *In Dahomey: A Negro Musical Comedy* on Broadway in 1903. Later, he founded the New York Syncopated Orchestra, playing jazz and ragtime, and toured with it in Europe.

Bert Williams and George Walker, who were stars of *In Dahomey*, formed a vaudeville duo, taking the parts of the sad blackface victim and the scheming city slicker but subverting the "coon" formula of White vaudeville. Despite being African Americans, they both played in blackface, using burnt cork as makeup. They both recorded extensively. Williams made history by joining the otherwise all-White cast of *Ziegfield Follies*, in which he was a huge success, and then teaming up with the White comedian Leon Errol in a new duo.

Ragtime capitalized on the increasing availability of pianos in middle class homes, and it created a major new star, Scott Joplin, the "King of Ragtime Writers." His music uses a "ragged" syncopated tune, with a left hand walking bass giving the rhythm, in line with traditional ragtime. However, he used his classical compositional training to create much more ambitious music than the "honky-tonk" ragtime heard in most saloons, using modulation (changing keys) to create greater harmonic richness.

Joplin saw ragtime as a serious musical form. He refused to perform in blackface and use comical dialect or racial stereotypes. But he gained a huge audience for his music, abandoning Victorian respectability and giving rhythmic drive and vitality to the dance.

James Reese Europe started as a ragtime musician; he was born in Alabama, grew up in Washington D.C., then migrated to New York in 1900. There, he helped create the Clef Club and led its orchestra. The club became a source of regular bookings for many Black musicians and featured the turkey trot and other "barnyard" dances.

Reese went to war in Europe with the Harlem Hellfighters, where he led the 369th Infantry Regiment's band. On his return, he pivoted from ragtime to jazz, then to a very new style. He saw jazz as a typically African American tradition and a source of Black pride. His first recordings, though, were made in France, with Pathé Records, where his lively syncopated "Memphis blues" sparked a ragtime craze. He made it home from France only to be stabbed by a band member in 1919. If he had not died so young, he would surely have been one of the greats of the jazz and blues pantheon.

The blues was created in the South around 1890/1900 and is a powerful statement of Southern African American life, with great emotional power and directness. The harmonic form is very simple, and often, the melodies feel pentatonic. It makes great use of "blue" notes, tones that are deliberately pitched flat to give an off-key feel. Early blues used vocal effects such as sliding, growling, and shouting—far from the European tradition of lyrical song—and often used African American proverbs such as "You reap what you sow," and "You never miss the water 'til your well runs dry."

The first generation of (Mississippi) Delta blues artists sang in juke joints and needed day jobs to make a living. Son House, one of these early blues artists, first recorded in 1930, but his career only took off when he was "rediscovered" in the 1960s during the American folk music revival. Lead Belly had to work as a driver for folk music collector John Lomax to pay his way during the Great Depression. Robert Johnson, despite the rumor he'd made a pact with the devil—his soul for his guitar technique—used to busk on street corners and spent his entire life (a short one) on the road.

In the 1930s and '40s, the blues spread to the North, taken by musicians like Muddy Waters and Howlin' Wolf, who moved from Mississippi to Chicago. While Delta blues had always been acoustic, electric guitar soon made an impact on the Chicago blues style, using distortion and overdrive to create a new, urban sound—one that would have a major impact on the development of early rock music.

The different styles of Black music were never exclusive. Many jazz greats got started playing to accompany blues singers. Mamie Smith sang both jazz and blues and was the first African American artist to record the blues, beginning the era of classic female blues that was continued by Ma Rainey, Bessie Smith (no relation), Esther Bigeou, and Ethel Waters. Gospel singer Mahalia Jackson remembers these blues records as all-pervasive during her New Orleans childhood. Black railroad porters would buy the records in the North and sell them for higher prices further south down the line.

Again, White entrepreneurs cashed in. Harry Pace founded Black Swan records in 1920 to try to keep African American music in the hands of a Black-owned company. He hired Ethel Waters rather than Bessie Smith to create a more dignified and classic style of blues. (Bessie had an earthier style of performance.) However, the company lasted only two years. The insurance company he founded as his next venture was much more successful.

Jazz came into being at the same time as the blues. In a sense, it blends the soul of the blues with the rhythm and drive of ragtime. New Orleans was the birthplace of jazz, blending creole musical traditions with the French style of brass band. The banjo and drums were joined by the clarinet, cornet, trombone, and piano.

Ferdinand LaMothe, better known as Jelly Roll Morton, a Creole piano player, claimed to have invented jazz. That claim might be exaggerated, but he was one of the greats of the New Orleans school, melding shout with ragtime to create a swinging, lively new style. But soon, as with blues, jazz joined the Great Migration, heading for Chicago and New York. Louis Armstrong, singer and trumpeter, moved from the South to Chicago and then New York, where he moved the New York big band style evolved by James Reese Europe toward a more improvisational form. Even Jelly Roll eventually moved north.

Sidney Bechet, sax and clarinet player, grew up in New Orleans and worked with Louis Armstrong to create the "swing" style, which pulled jazz away from its ragtime roots. Together with Armstrong, he developed improvisation as a key element of jazz, using scales, arpeggios, and varying melodies to show off his instrumental skills. Swing brought rhythmic freedom into the music, escaping from the frenetic tempo of ragtime and often putting notes before or after the beat. It was sensual music that symbolized the jazz age's desire for freedom from stifling conformity and respectability. It was also incredibly danceable.

Louis Armstrong also popularized "scat," which was probably derived from Black folk traditions. Scat is a form of vocal improvisation using nonsense syllables, sometimes imitating instruments: diga diga, boop-boop-a-doop, hi-dee-hi-dee ha-di-da, or be-bop-a-lula. Ella Fitzgerald later became a great scat singer. Scat gave singers the same freedom to improvise as instrumentalists, setting them free from the lyrics.

A pivotal figure in the history of jazz with his fifty-year career, Duke Ellington was born in Washington, D.C., but moved to New York in 1923. He soon became part of the Harlem Renaissance, dominating the swing era as a composer, pianist, and bandleader. As a "New Negro," his idea was to portray African American experience through music, and his works often have racially meaningful titles such as "Black and Tan Fantasy." Jazz in the 1930s had become a global phenomenon, allowing African American musicians to travel the world. Duke Ellington toured Europe with his band, meeting classical musicians as well as jazz fans. He began to write extended compositions, such as "Creole Rhapsody" and "Black, Brown and Beige."

While Duke Ellington's swing had taken off in Europe, in 1930s America it was still often seen as "Black" music attracting a mainly African American audience. And Jim Crow laws made touring the South difficult. Duke Ellington solved this problem in a typically stylish way by hiring a private train that could serve as a hotel and restaurant for his band.

If Ellington was a duke, Ella Fitzgerald was the queen of jazz. Though born in Virginia, she was brought up in New York. After a deprived childhood, she was eventually asked to join Chick Webb's orchestra, which performed at the Savoy Ballroom in Harlem. This was her springboard to stardom. In 1938, she had her first hit with the band: "A-Tisket, A-Tasket," a song she had co-written.

The 1940s marked the decline of swing and the beginnings of bebop, a more abstract music that was less driven by danceability and could explore advanced harmonies and complex rhythms. Big bands were out, and small combos ruled the roost. Working now with Dizzy Gillespie's band, Ella started to explore scat singing, and for a while, her career was entirely based on bebop. But in the late '50s, she began to record the Great American Songbook, blending jazz standards, show tunes, and popular songs and attracting an audience that bebop could not reach.

The exuberance and joy of Ella Fitzgerald's singing was matched by her commitment to civil rights. She asked venues to ensure there was no racial segregation of the audience and worked with Norm Granz, a fervent anti-racist, as her manager. She also collaborated with almost all the jazz greats: Duke Ellington, Louis Armstrong, Count Basie, and Oscar Peterson, just to name a few.

With bebop, younger Harlem musicians took the lead: pianist Thelonious Monk, trumpeters Dizzy Gillespie and Miles Davis, sax player Charlie Parker, and pianist Bud Powell. Their greater use of dissonance, more recherché harmonies, quicker tempos, and "cutting contests" that set instrumentalist against each other (similar to battle rap today) made bebop into music for listening rather than for dancing. At the same time, White musicians like saxophonist Stan Getz, drummer Stan Levey, and sax player Aaron Sachs were getting involved in bebop.

Postwar jazz featured two major talents: Miles Davis, working as a composer as well as trumpeter in a huge range of work, and sax player John Coltrane. Both expanded the field of jazz. Davis developed harmonically rich sound pictures with a striking new sensibility, creating "cool" jazz, while Coltrane focused on spiritual exploration with heavily modal work (that is, working outside the regular key structure). Miles Davis found he was treated better in Europe than in the US, at one point working in France with French jazz musicians.

Gospel music blends the tradition of African American spirituals with the expressive possibilities of jazz and blues. It stands at the core of most Black Protestant churches and benefited from the Pentecostal strain in African American worship, which included speaking in tongues and handling snakes. In the Azusa Street revival in early twentieth-century Los Angeles, moans, shouts, and energetic dancing joined the singing of hymns. There was also a lot of influence from the blues.

Sister Rosetta Tharpe, one of the earliest leading figures of gospel music, started recording in 1938, playing electric guitar and using heavy distortion. She was willing to play in nightclubs and concert halls as well as in churches and incorporated blues and jazz influences into her music. However, her influence went beyond gospel. She would eventually be a huge influence on rock and roll, particularly through her tour in Britain in 1964.

Mahalia Jackson, a student of Thomas A. Dorsey's, had been singing for fifteen years before she burst on to the national scene in 1947 with "Move On Up a Little Higher." Her voice was low, powerful, and had a huge range, and she had a strong stage presence that let her sing with intense emotion. She included jazz and blues influences in her singing, using "blue notes" and bending her pitch frequently, often improvising and varying the melody. She moaned, hummed, crooned, hollered, and shouted—though she had studied the vocal technique of classical singers through recordings. (She never learned to read music.) But despite the mixed nature of her style, she was never willing to sing in nightclubs or concert halls.

Mahalia was a strong supporter of the civil rights movement, often singing for fundraisers; she also sang at the March on Washington. By 1963, she was an international celebrity and sang at Kennedy's inauguration. Her style eventually influenced R&B and early rock and roll, and her use of the Hammond organ was copied by many popular musicians.

Soul music grew out of the gospel tradition, blending it with jazz and R&B influences. Catchy rhythms, handclaps, and call and response forms make it very easy music to relate to. While jazz was becoming color-blind, soul remained a distinctively African American music despite a handful of "blue-eyed soul" acts—more in the UK than the US.

The blind pianist and singer Ray Charles was a pioneer of soul. He added sexuality to the gospel sound, his "What'd I say" even being banned by some radio stations for its suggestive lyrics. He stretched his voice to falsetto range in some songs, descended to a bass in others, and used all the armory of gospel shouts, wails, and moans in his emotionally intense performance. He added female vocal backing to the soul sound and remained close to R&B and jazz, often performing across these genres.

James Brown was a flamboyant character full of macho energy who danced frenetically while he sang. He had been raised in a brothel, spent time in jail, and was involved in the Black Power movement—his "Say It Loud, I'm Black and I'm Proud" became its anthem. He played with a huge band, performing over 300 shows a year, and was nicknamed "Mr. Dynamite" and "the Hardest-Working Man in Show Business." Like Ray Charles, he used shouts, grunts, and shrieks as well as his singing voice to communicate the intensity of his music. Eventually, his music developed toward funk, a hypnotic style with a slow tempo and a complex percussive groove.

But, just as women were at the heart of gospel music, so soul also had its queen: Aretha Franklin, whose roots lay in gospel. She was the daughter of a well-known preacher and friend of Martin Luther King Jr.'s, and Mahalia Jackson was a friend of the family. While she started her career singing a mix of different genres such as jazz, R&B, and pop, Atlantic Records producer Jerry Wexler encouraged her to concentrate on soul, where her gospel background would give her an advantage.

She dominated the 1960s and 1970s, and in 1972 returned to gospel with the album *Amazing Grace*. Her voice and musicianship were phenomenal. When Luciano Pavarotti was unable to sing "Nessun Dorma" at the 1998 Grammy Awards, she stepped in and sang it in full tenor voice—but in her own inimitable style.

Blues, meanwhile, had developed into rhythm and blues—R&B—adding an insistent beat while retaining the twelve-bar chord progression typical of the blues. Cuban rhythms were added to the mix. With the advent of soul music, R&B had acquired the ecstatic vibes of gospel. Adding the electric guitar to the mix created the conditions under which rock and roll began to emerge. Unlike jazz, which had moved toward ever greater flexibility, R&B added a driving rhythm and backbeat.

Rock and roll music started being played in the late 1940s, and in the 1950s, Chuck Berry took up the new style and broke through to mainstream pop. Atypical for a Black artist, he appealed to White teens as well as to the "race records" market with his raw sound, immense guitar riffs, and showmanship. Little Richard was another pioneer of rock and roll, incorporating the wailing voice of gospel music into his performances. His makeup, glittering costumes, and rebellious character had a huge impact on the image of rock musicians.

When Elvis Presley came on the scene in 1954, he was singing "Black music." Thereafter, rock developed into a predominantly White musical form. By the time Jimi Hendrix came to play at Woodstock in 1969, he was practically the only Black musician there. In a folk music and progressive rock world full of White boys, he stood out—an astonishingly innovative player. Like many African Americans, he saw his career take off when he started playing overseas, experiencing huge success in England with his furiously passionate guitar style.

A major event in the history of African American music was the launch of Motown Records in 1959. Founder Berry Gordy focused on soul with R&B elements, creating a very "clean" sound compared to gospel shouting or rock music, with an optimistic vibe. Acts included the Four Tops, the Temptations, Marvin Gaye, Stevie Wonder, and The Supremes with Diana Ross. In the 1970s, Motown got involved in protest soul music but retained a popular, feel-good style.

Blues Royalties

African American musicians have often been exploited. Some have seen recording companies take the lion's share of their earnings. Often, White musicians have taken on Black musical styles without giving any recognition to their sources. But it's not always like that. Folklore collector and musicologist Alan Lomax once recorded James Carter, then a prisoner, lead the singing of "Po Lazarus," a slow blues song. The song became well known, and years later, it was used as part of the soundtrack of the film *O Brother, Where Art Thou?*

James Carter disappeared. But the leaders of the Lomax Digital Archive kept trying to find him. Eventually, they managed to trace him. To his surprise, they gave him a plaque celebrating the two millionth sale of the recording, plus all his past royalties.

No history of African American music would be complete without mentioning Michael Jackson, who grew out of Motown and his family ensemble The Jackson Five to become a major solo act and produce the best-selling album of all time, *Thriller* (1982). He drew on influences as diverse as Motown artists, funk, disco, rock, rap, and jazz. His producer, Quincy Jones, was not only a jazz trumpeter but a student of French classical composer Nadia Boulanger.

Notably, Jackson used video and spectacle to a degree rarely seen before, taking full advantage of the opportunity offered by the relatively young music cable channel MTV to transform the music video into an art form of its own. His career broke out of the "race music" silo to make him the prime pop musician of his day, forever demolishing the barriers between African American music and White consumers and media.

Much of his music has humanitarian themes, though there is also a dark, paranoid, and dystopian feel to some of his work. "Black or White" (a triple platinum single) references Zulu dance, the KKK, and the Statue of Liberty to convey a message about racial harmony; his "They Don't Care About Us" is a straightforward African American protest song (though it became controversial due to an allegedly anti-Semitic chorus).

A new style rooted in the African American community broke through in the last quarter of the twentieth century: hip-hop, including rapping. It may have been influenced by the Jamaican tradition of deejay toasting (talking over a rhythm track) and grew up in the 1970s Bronx, where Latino and African American youth were involved in hip-hop culture. Graffiti, beatboxing, and breakdancing were all part of this culture.

Hip-hop is a counterculture, defining itself as opposed to authority. Grandmaster Flash rapped about police brutality, while Public Enemy put out tracks entitled "Don't Believe the Hype" and "Fight the Power." The 1980s and 1990s were good for the African American middle class but bad for urban youth, who suffered from racial profiling by police and high unemployment. Hip-hop became a powerful force for them to express their concerns. (It's interesting that rap has been adopted by minorities like Algerians in France to protest racism and poverty.)

However, rap has been accused of gender bias and even misogyny. Lyrics from rappers such as Snoop Dogg and Dr. Dre portray women in a sexualized and objectivized way, frequently describing violence against women. More recently, female rappers have appeared, such as Queen Latifah, Salt-N-Pepa, and TLC.

African American music is still developing, with current African American artists including best-selling Beyoncé, flute player and singer Lizzo, and Lil Nas X, a gay rapper who has broken new ground for LGBTQ+ African Americans with his coming out.

The popular music world of today was very largely created by African Americans, a contribution that hasn't always been recognized but is getting increasing attention from both musicians and music historians. It's safe to say that without African American music, today's musical world would look very different. There would have been no Beatles and no Rolling Stones. John Lennon, talking to *JET* magazine, said that when the Beatles arrived in the US in 1964, their musical idols were Little Richard, Chuck Berry, and Bo Diddley. "Black music was my life, and still is," he said.[i]

---

[i] "JET: Ex-Beatle Tells How Black Stars Changed His Life," *JET*, October 26, 1972, https://www.johnlennon.com/news/jet-ex-beatle-tells-how-black-stars-changed-his-life/.

Chapter 9: Voting Rights and Black Lives Matter

Although this book has traced centuries of progress for African Americans, the civil rights struggle is still ongoing. Racial justice and equality has not yet been fully achieved.

Jim Crow may not have come back, but voter suppression certainly has. For more than a decade, increased Black voter participation after the civil rights revolution of the 1960s has been reversing, according to the Brennan Center for Justice. New voter laws are being brought in, and largely unsubstantiated allegations of voting fraud have led to calls for tightening up the law and mass challenges to voters.

A study from the Brennan Center shows that it has mainly been Republicans who support such legislation, and that legislators' sponsorship of such laws closely correlates with the racial makeup of their district. This is part of a pattern of "racial backlash." White Americans feel that their power has been undermined by minorities' increasing representation in politics and economic power and are trying to dilute the minority's voting rights as a response.[i]

---

[i] Kevin Morris, "Patterns in the Introduction and Passage of Restrictive Voting Bills Are Best Explained By Race," Brennan Center for Justice, August 3, 2022, https://www.brennancenter.org/our-work/research-reports/patterns-introduction-and-passage-restrictive-voting-bills-are-best.

Mass challenges to voters, together with more frequent purges of registration data, are most often directed against African American and Hispanic voters. Many conservatives are using Eagle AI to deliver data for mass challenges, for instance. Mass challenges may seem democratic, but oddly enough, they are often focused on precincts with large communities of African Americans, Hispanics, or registered Democrats. The inability of eligible voters to vote from jail (when they are held pre-trial, for instance, or have been convicted of a misdemeanor, not a felony) also hits African Americans hard—particularly young African American voters.

The requirement to show certain types of identification may not seem racist but can have a disproportionate effect on marginalized communities. Twenty-one percent of African Americans lack a driver's license, compared to only 8 percent of the White population, and nearly 14 percent of Black households don't have a checking account. (Native Americans and transgender individuals also have major problems with obtaining adequate, up-to-date IDs.)

In the 2000 presidential election, George Bush won the state of Florida by just 537 votes in the face of many African Americans being wrongly purged from registration rolls. The Commission on Civil Rights found that there was no conspiracy to deprive voters of their rights, but that Florida officials had turned a blind eye to the fact that increased voter registration and aging voting systems had put intense pressure on the system.

Voter purges are intended to remove the registrations of voters who have moved or died. In the last two decades, though, purge rates have increased substantially and may now be disenfranchising many eligible voters. For instance, a voter might be purged if they have ordered their mail to be forwarded, even though they may just be in hospital, at college, or on a temporary work assignment.

The software used for purging is also important. ERIC, used by many states, uses a sophisticated matching system that includes hashed and encrypted social security numbers, driver's license data, death records, and USPS change of address data. It also facilitates new registrations, for instance when a voter has moved state. However, it is now a target of the Republican Right. Nine Republican-led states have stopped using it.

A system called Crosscheck is sometimes used instead. However, because it only checks first and last names, it is likely to purge valid voters. This is particularly dangerous in communities where certain first and last names are disproportionately common. (As of 2019, this system was suspended as the result of a lawsuit by the ACLU.)

Another way to dilute the strength of the African American vote is gerrymandering—the biased redrawing of precinct and district lines. Redistricting must be done every so often as migration and demographics change the population of particular areas. However, gerrymandering manipulates the redistricting process for a political advantage. Two techniques known as "cracking" and "packing" are used. Cracking splits up voters across different districts to weaken their power, while packing aims to pack a group into a single district, consequently weakening their power in other districts.

For instance, in Nashville, the city was divided among three Republican-leaning districts ("cracking"). This effectively destroyed a safe Democrat seat. The same happened in Atlanta, Georgia. The Brennan Center estimates that, while Republicans aren't the only ones to use these techniques, gerrymandering gives them a sixteen-seat advantage in congressional elections.

Another focus of African American concern is police brutality. In the early 1990s, the Rodney King case caught national attention. Amateur videographer George Holliday witnessed four White Los Angeles Police Department officers beating King and decided to video the scene from his apartment. The video was repeatedly played on broadcast news. Despite this evidence, a majority White jury (containing no African Americans, one Latino, and one Asian) acquitted the four White officers of using excessive force. Riots in Los Angeles lasted for six days after the trial verdict was delivered, killing over sixty people and resulting in tremendous damage to property.

President George Bush ordered the Department of Justice to consider filing charges on the basis that King's civil rights had been violated. At this second trial, two of the officers were convicted. The case showed that despite the progress made in the '50s and '60s, there was still something very wrong about African Americans' place in American society. Black and White citizens had contrasting experiences of and views about the government and justice system; their Americas were different places. Many Black Americans referred to a new offence that was being policed, although it wasn't on the statute book: DWB, "Driving While Black" (a parody of Driving While Intoxicated).

Police brutality hit the headlines again in the twenty-first century, and in response, a new mass movement arose. In 2013, after George Zimmerman was acquitted of murdering Black teenager Trayvon Martin, activists created the Twitter hashtag #BlackLivesMatter (BLM). This became the first major civil rights organization in the era of social media, and in 2020, it went mainstream after the death of George Floyd at the hands of a Minneapolis police officer. Fifteen to twenty-six million people participated in protests across the world, including Hispanics and Asian Americans, with 60 percent support in 2020 even among White Americans.

Social media enabled BLM to be managed in a decentralized manner, with grassroots, local action. An online platform provided a network that could be used by activists. Social media also allowed bystanders to easily video police violence and post the videos on social media. George Holliday would be joined by hundreds of other video makers in calling the police to account.

BLM brought many young people who had never taken political action before into the movement. It also renewed the idea of community control by the community, for the community, with its calls to defund the police and allow communities to decide their own policing priorities.

But while BLM was something quite new, it reconnected with the continual struggle for civil rights— from the Civil War and the Fourteenth and Fifteenth Amendment to the 1960s civil rights movement. In particular, the singing of "Lift Ev'ry Voice and Sing" at BLM marches, with its rousing final line, "Let us march on 'til victory is won" was a direct reference to the 1950s and 1960s era of protest. So were "die-ins," modeled after the lunch counter sit-ins of the 1950s.

The NAACP hasn't gone away, though. It has 425,000 members and has broadened its remit to "eliminate race-based discrimination." Recently, it scored a public relations coup by issuing travel advisories, counseling people of color to avoid Missouri (in 2017) and Florida (in 2023), and giving its reasoning. It actively educates and mentors the next generation of leadership and pursues equitable health systems, educational opportunities, and economics.

Late NAACP chairman Julian Bond also supported marriage equality, comparing the struggle for gay rights to the struggle for African Americans' civil rights. "Sexual disposition parallels race," he said in a 2005 speech. "I was born this way. I have no choice. I wouldn't change it if I could."[i] In 2012, the NAACP board of directors decided to back gay marriage. In 2018, it invited LGBTQ+ activists to its 109th annual convention, and Chairman Leon W. Russell apologized for the organization's previously homophobic stance.

Black History Month has had a huge impact in making African Americans and other ethnicities aware of the troubled past of African Americans and their contributions to society. The discipline has grown in universities, but Black History Month takes the story of African Americans into schools, libraries, and cultural centers and brings greater public awareness. Carter G. Woodson, the "Father of Black History" and himself the son of formerly enslaved parents, founded Negro History Week in 1926, which later expanded to Black History Month in February.

Recently, partly because of BLM, the call for reparations has been made. Slavery and the Jim Crow era created ongoing disparities in wealth and education and even a lower life expectancy for African Americans. Those who support reparations claim that the nation should compensate the current generation of African Americans in what writer Ta-Nehisi Coates has called "a national reckoning."

Reparations might involve compensation to individuals along the lines of the "forty acres and a mule" promised by General Sherman to former slaves. But the real aim of reparations would be to create an economic empowerment package for African Americans. This might involve establishing Black-owned media, a national program for teaching Black history, a loan program for first-time home buyers, or the creation of a Black Land Bank. Some higher education institutions that benefited from slavery have already established reparation funds. Georgetown University now provides $400,000 a year to community projects that will benefit the descendants of those enslaved on Jesuit plantations in Maryland.

Going beyond reparations, some African Americans are proposing a new political relationship between Black people and the United States, which might be modeled after that of Indigenous nations. Black communities could have a similar status to First Peoples' Reservations

---

[i] Eartha Melzer, "NAACP Chair Says 'Gay Rights Are Civil Rights,'" *Washington Blade*, April 8, 2005. https://web.archive.org/web/20060321202124/http://www.washblade.com/2005/4-8/news/localnews/naacp.cfm.

and self-govern while retaining existing political rights within the US. This remains controversial, but it reflects the fact that many African Americans feel that the impact of slavery and racial discrimination has not yet been completely eradicated from their lives.

In the twenty-first century, a lot of historically White institutions have looked again at how inequality benefited them. Many have found that they profited from slavery, perhaps directly or indirectly through donations given them by slave owners. The University of Cambridge was already investigating how its finances were linked to transatlantic slavery, and the BLM movement made this research increasingly topical.

Harvard University published its own report in 2022, showing that Harvard and its staff had enslaved more than seventy people directly and invested in the West Indies and Southern cotton plantations that employed slaves. Harvard pledged $100 million to fund reparation efforts, such as deepening links with historically Black colleges and universities. Since slavery in New England included the enslavement of Indigenous Americans, Harvard will also support Native American communities, students, and research.

Chapter 10: A Colored Legacy: Reflections and Hope for the Future

Where are we now? Politically, African Americans are now well represented in the House, with 157 African American representatives. In 2022, there were more than 640 Black mayors.[i] At other levels, less progress has been made. There have still been only eleven Black US senators. Hiram Revels, the first, took his oath of office in 1870—with poetic justice, replacing Jefferson Davis, formerly president of the Confederacy. Currently, there are just three Black senators and only one Black governor, Wes Moore, of Maryland.

In 2008, America at last elected an African American to the highest office, with Barack Obama becoming president and re-elected for a second term in 2012. Many Black Americans could hardly believe it was possible that Obama's campaign had succeeded. (However, "birther" opposition, which claimed Obama had not been born in the United States and was ineligible for office, showed that racism was still alive and well in some quarters.)

---

[i] Jabari Simama, "Black Elected Officials and the Nuanced Issue of Expectations," *Governing*, March 29, 2022. https://www.governing.com/now/black-elected-officials-and-the-nuanced-issue-of-expectations.

Notably, Obama galvanized the grassroots and young people with his slogan "Yes we can"—originally used by his friend Deval Patrick in his successful fight to become Massachusetts' first Black governor. But Obama also sought the alliance of White voters. When video clips of his pastor railing against White America were published, he explained the context of America's conflicted racial history and noted that a solution "requires all Americans to realize that your dreams do not have to come at the expense of my dreams."[1]

Increasingly, African Americans share their Blackness with Afro-Latinos and Afro-Caribbeans; Blackness is not monolithic. Kamala Harris, Democratic nominee for the presidency in 2024, is of Afro-Jamaican and Indian parentage. Obama, too, was of mixed parentage. Intersectionality is no longer an advanced notion but a necessary part of getting to grips with a changing world. Still, most African Americans have slavery in their family tree—something they do not share with Black populations in places like the UK, France, or Africa.

African American creativity continues to make a huge contribution to American culture. While Black actors in the past struggled to get roles that weren't stereotyped, Samuel L. Jackson, Morgan Freeman, Will Smith, Forest Whitaker, and Denzel Washington have all had successful careers. Halle Berry became the first African American woman to win an Academy Award for her role in *Monster's Ball*, and Queen Latifah has combined rap and mainstream musical success with a film and TV acting career. There have even been rumors that Black British actor Idris Elba could be the next James Bond, which would have been unthinkable a few decades ago. Black directors like Spike Lee, Steve McQueen (a British citizen) and Ava DuVernay have helped create films that speak to African American audiences, such as *Do the Right Thing*, *Twelve Years a Slave*, and *Selma*.

The historic African American contribution to US history and culture is now being recognized after decades of being overlooked. The story of rock and roll, for instance, had been "whitewashed" in many accounts of popular music, but the contribution of late 1940s Black artists like the Ink Spots and Joe Turner, as well as Little Richard and Chuck Berry in the 1950s, is now being rediscovered.

---

[1] "Transcript: Barack Obama's Speech on Race," March 18, 2008, CBS News. https://www.cbsnews.com/news/transcript-barack-obamas-speech-on-race/.

The "New Negroes" of the Harlem Renaissance would have approved the increasing reclamation of African Americans' culture and African roots. Scholar Henry Louis Gates Jr., at Harvard, used genetic testing and genealogical research in his TV series *African American Lives* to take celebrities like Oprah Winfrey, Quincy Jones, Mae Jemison, and Whoopi Goldberg back to their roots, first in the Southern states and then in Africa.

Faith Ringgold took African American quilts in a new direction, storytelling through the quilt medium and focusing on Black American life, including the experience of racism. At the same time, the authentic tradition of the Gee's Bend quilters in Alabama became better known, with a series of major exhibitions from 2002 onward.

African American writers (as well as Brits and Nigerians) have used Africanfuturism to imagine a Black future. N.K. Jemisin and Nnedi Okorafor have become particularly prominent in the science fiction world. In the mainstream, African superhero Black Panther's story has been examined in the films *Black Panther* and *Wakanda Forever*, directed by African American Ryan Coogler.

In *Wakanda Forever*, Wakanda is a vision of a technologically advanced Africa. Its capital is a smart city where thatched roofs combine with high-rise buildings and maglev trains, and high tech overlaps with worship of a Yoruba-style pantheon that includes ancient Egyptian deities. The films used southern African costume elements such as Basotho blankets, beadwork, and Zulu headdresses, put together by an African American designer who had also worked on Spike Lee's *Do the Right Thing*. (Ruth E. Carter became the first Black person to win an Oscar for costume design with her work on *Black Panther*; she won the award again for the second film.)

African Americans now have several holidays that bring them together as a community. One is the celebration of Kwanzaa from December 26 to January 1, which was first observed in 1966. Kwanzaa is based on African harvest traditions and the values of unity, self-determination, collective responsibility, cooperative economics, purpose, creativity, and faith. Candles represent these seven principles of community, and ears of corn are set out for each child in a family. In 1997, the US Postal Service issued a Kwanzaa stamp.

The festival reflects the growing desire of African Americans to develop their own identity in the same way Irish Americans, for instance, celebrate St Patrick's Day and often retain an affection for "the old country." (Interestingly, it is estimated that over a third of African Americans have some Irish ancestry; they are now linked by the African American Irish Diaspora Network.)

In 1983, President Reagan made Martin Luther King Jr. Day, the third Monday in January, a national holiday. However, some states did not celebrate it. The last holdout was New Hampshire, which had its first MLK Day in 2000. Some Southern states hold a joint commemoration for King and for Confederate General Robert E. Lee—rubbing salt into African American wounds.

Juneteenth, the nineteenth of June, was for a long time an informal holiday celebrating the end of slavery in the US and the final enforcement of the Emancipation Proclamation in Texas in 1865. President Biden made it a federal holiday in 2021. It is now formally recognized in every state and seen by many African Americans as a "second Independence Day."

But there are still major issues facing the African American community, and these holidays should help motivate activism for future change as well as celebration for past success. In some areas, the effect of pervasive racism is only just being noticed. For instance, there are major health issues affecting the Black population. Black women are three times more likely than White women to die in childbirth, and sudden infant death syndrome is twice as prevalent with African American babies. African Americans are also more likely to be severely impacted by diabetes, asthma, and heart disease, and during the Covid pandemic, Black mortality was much higher than among other ethnicities.

While some of these issues may reflect the lower economic standing of many African Americans, healthcare issues also reflect the fact that clinical trials have historically used mainly White subjects. Research is therefore White-biased, and medications are developed that may not have the desired effect on Black patients.

While *Brown v. Board of Education* managed to overturn *Plessy v. Ferguson* with the argument that segregated education damages the self-esteem of Black pupils, high suicide rates for Black teens show that the experience of racism is still traumatic for many African Americans.

And there are new threats on the horizon. Artificial intelligence (AI) is increasingly being used as a way of automating decisions in both public and private sector institutions. Because AI replicates existing norms, racism and other prejudices are built into it. And because of a lack of diversity in some tech firms' hiring practices, these biases aren't challenged—indeed, they may not even be noticed.

AI biases could put people of color at risk of increased problems with the Transportation Security Administration (TSA) when they are flying, increased likelihood of banks turning them down for loans, and decreased visibility on social media and content networks. These are tomorrow's battles for African Americans. The fight isn't over yet!

But history shows that these battles can be won and that African Americans have the keys to their future in their hands. The fight for justice and equality continues, for African Americans, for other people of color, and for their White allies. Looking at the legacy that great African Americans like Frederick Douglass, W.E.B. Du Bois, Rosa Parks, Malcolm X, and Martin Luther King Jr. have left should serve as an inspiration for a future that honors their example and delivers equity for their inheritors.

W.E.B. Du Bois, in a 1919 editorial for *The Crisis*, welcomed African American soldiers home with a rousing battle cry, and it's still valid today: "We return. We return from fighting. We return fighting.

Make way for democracy. We saved it in France, and by the Great Jehovah, we will save it in the United States of America, or know the reason why."[i]

---

[i] Courtland Cox and Charles Cob, "Protest, Race, and the American Future," *The Crisis*, July 1, 2020, https://naacp.org/articles/protest-race-and-american-future.

Conclusion

Try to understand what America would be like without African Americans. There would be no jazz. No rock and roll. No soul or R&B. No hot sauce. No gumbo. No dirty rice. Probably no rice at all. (It was Africans who taught the French how to grow it in Louisiana.) More seriously, the United States would have a much smaller economy because Black people have done a lot of the work, from the plantations to the Detroit automobile factories. It would also have no traffic lights and quite likely no subways. Man might not have reached the moon without the African American contribution to the math and computing side of the space program. Maybe the Russians would be the only nation to have made it into space. What is certain is that the world would be a very, very different place without the African American contribution.

And yet throughout the entire history of America, African Americans have had to fight for their freedom, for the right to vote, and for equal education and access to public spaces, the law, and political representation. They have had to fight against public institutions that wanted to exclude them, against misinformation, stereotypes, prejudice, and economic disadvantage. That history of activism continues today, inspired by the history of individual and collective resistance to injustice.

One of the most impressive things about the history of African Americans is that the search for freedom and justice has so often been linked to the determination to become better human beings, whether through education, the Christian religion, or Islam. Individual and collective empowerment have always been linked. In the history of Black music, for instance, it's impressive how often jazz stars used their own prominence to fight for civil rights—demanding unsegregated audiences, singing at civil rights fundraisers or marches, or promoting other African American musicians.

Black Americans have also had strong White allies when it counted. Marilyn Monroe determined to help her friend Ella Fitzgerald get a gig at the Mocambo—she promised to take a table at the front of the house every night that Ella sang there. She kept her word, and Frank Sinatra and Judy Garland also turned up to the opening night. Anthoine (Anthony) Benezet, a Protestant exile from France, was a refugee who became one of the first American abolitionists and founded a school for African American girls. Eleanor Roosevelt was a true friend to African Americans, resigning from the Daughters of the American Revolution when they refused to let Black contralto Marian Anderson sing in Washington's Constitution Hall.

Of course, the African American story isn't *about* White allies. But it would be a mistake to overlook their contribution—not least because today, too, White people can make a difference simply by learning African American history and being personally committed to act for racial justice.

In the same way, many African Americans have broadened their vision to include other dispossessed people and victims of colonialism or fascism in their struggle. African Americans fought against fascism in Europe, got involved in the Bandung Conference, and have helped Native Americans in their own fight for justice. Malcolm X reached out to Muslims in the Middle East and Africa; W.E.B. Du Bois was a leader of the Pan-African movement and spent a lifetime opposing anti-Semitism. Far from looking after number one, these great African Americans had the generosity of spirit to oppose racism and injustice everywhere.

That's why Black history should be an inspiration for everyone. The struggle isn't over yet!

Here's another book by Enthralling History that you might like

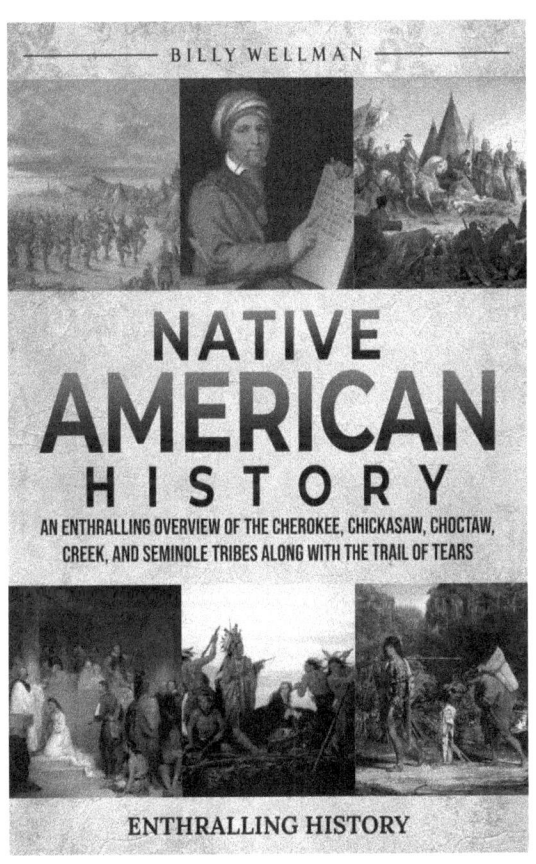

Free limited time bonus

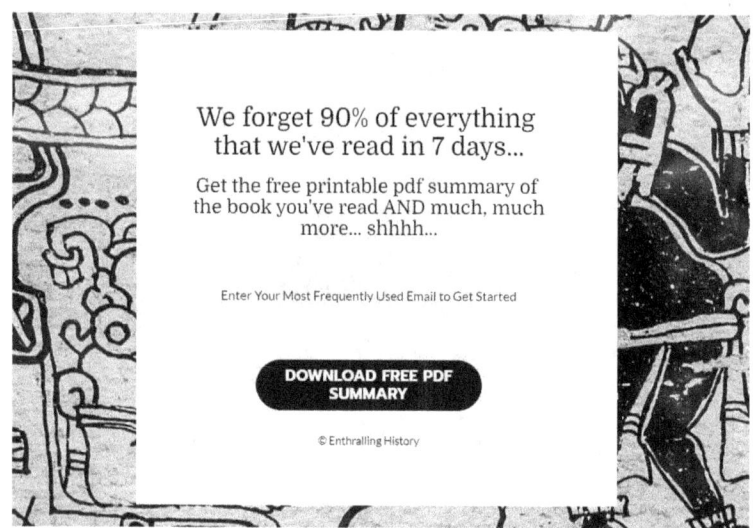

Stop for a moment. We have a free bonus set up for you. The problem is this: we forget 90% of everything that we read after 7 days. Crazy fact, right? Here's the solution: we've created a printable, 1-page pdf summary for this book that you're reading now. All you have to do to get your free pdf summary is to go to the following website:
https://livetolearn.lpages.co/enthrallinghistory/

Or, Scan the QR code!

Once you do, it will be intuitive. Enjoy, and thank you!

Bibliography and Further Reading

Bethune, Mary McLeod. "Clarifying Our Vision with the Facts." *Journal of Negro History* 23, no. 1 (1938): 10-15. https://doi.org/10.2307/2714703.

Bibb, Henry. *Life and Adventures of an American Slave*. Madison, Wisconsin, 2001.

BlackPast.org. "(1963) Josephine Baker, 'Speech at the March on Washington.'" Accessed April 2, 2025. https://web.archive.org/web/20180920010915/http://www.blackpast.org/1963-josephine-baker-speech-march-washington.

Bower, Javacia Harris. "How Executives Hold Back Black Women at Work." *Her Money*, May 30, 2024. https://hermoney.com/earn/careers/how-executives-hold-black-women-back-at-work/.

Campbell, Barbara. "Black Feminists Form Group Here; National Body Hopes to End 'Myths' and Intimidation." *The New York Times*, August 16, 1973. https://www.census.gov/newsroom/press-releases/2023/annual-business-survey-employer-business-characteristics.html.

Carson, C., Lewis, D.L. "Martin Luther King, Jr." *Encyclopedia Britannica*, March 31, 2025. https://www.britannica.com/biography/Martin-Luther-King-Jr/The-Montgomery-bus-boycott.

CBS News. "Transcript: Barack Obama's Speech on Race," March 18, 2008. https://www.cbsnews.com/news/transcript-barack-obamas-speech-on-race/.

Clinton, Catherine. *Harriet Tubman: the Road to Freedom*. New York, 2004.

Cox, Courtland and Cobb, Charles. "Protest, Race, and the American Future." *The Crisis*, July 1, 2020. https://naacp.org/articles/protest-race-and-american-future.

Douglass, Frederick. "What to a Slave Is the Fourth of July?" Speech, July 5, 1852. The Ashbrook Center. Accessed April 2, 2025. https://teachingamericanhistory.org/document/what-to-the-slave-is-the-fourth-of-july-4/.

Equiano, Olaudah. *The Interesting Narrative of the Life of Olaudah Equiano, or Gustavus Vassa, the African*. London, 1789.

Franklin, J.H. and Higginbotham, E.B. *From Slavery to Freedom: A History of African Americans*. McGraw Hill, 2011.

Graham, Maryemma, and Ward, Jerry W. ed. *The Cambridge History of African American Literature*. Cambridge University Press 2011.

Haley, Alex, and Malcolm X. *The Autobiography of Malcolm X*. African American Images, 1969.

Hardin, Daniel. "Raging Civil Rights Struggle Leads to Union Victories: Cambridge MD 1938." Washington Area Spark. Accessed April 2, 2025. https://washingtonareaspark.com/tag/gloria-richardson/.

Harvard Radcliffe Institute. "Shirley Chisholm Addresses the National Women's Political Caucus." September 9, 2020. https://www.radcliffe.harvard.edu/news-and-ideas/shirley-chisholm-addresses-the-national-women-s-political-caucus.

Holmes, Keith C. *Black Inventors: Crafting Over 200 Years of Success*. Global Black Inventor Research Projects, 2008.

Hornsby, Alton. *A Companion to African American History*. Blackwell, 2005.Johnlennon.com. "*JET*: Ex-Beatle Tells How Black Stars Changed His Life," *JET*, October 26, 1972, https://www.johnlennon.com/news/jet-ex-beatle-tells-how-black-stars-changed-his-life/.

Jones, Howard. *Mutiny on the Amistad*. Oxford University Press, 1997.

King, Jr., Martin Luther. "Letter from a Birmingham Jail." University of Pennsylvania African Studies Center. Accessed April 2, 2025. africa.upenn.edu/Articles_Gen/Letter_Birmingham.html.

Macmillan Center for International and Area Studies at Yale. "Niagara's Declaration of Principles, 1905." Accessed April 2, 2025. https://macmillan.yale.edu/glc/niagaras-declaration-principles-1905

Melzer, Eartha. "NAACP Chair Says 'Gay Rights Are Civil Rights,'" *Washington Blade*, April 8, 2005. https://web.archive.org/web/20060321202124/http://www.washblade.com/2005/4-8/news/localnews/naacp.cfm.

Morain, Rick. "Breaking the Barrier." *Storm Lake Times Pilot*, April 27, 2022. https://www.stormlake.com/stories/breaking-the-barrier,50170.

Morris, Kevin. "Patterns in the Introduction and Passage of Restrictive Voting Bills Are Best Explained By Race," Brennan Center for Justice, August 3, 2022, https://www.brennancenter.org/our-work/research-reports/patterns-introduction-and-passage-restrictive-voting-bills-are-best.

National Archives. "Thomas Jefferson to John Wayles Eppes, 30 June 1820." Accessed April 2, 2025. https://founders.archives.gov/documents/Jefferson/03-16-02-0052.

National Archives. "Plessy v. Ferguson (1896)." Updated February 8, 2022. https://www.archives.gov/milestone-documents/plessy-v-ferguson.

National Park Service. "16th Street Baptist Church Bombing." Accessed April 2, 2025. https://www.nps.gov/articles/16thstreetbaptist.htm.

National Park Service. "Sojourner Truth: 'Ain't I a Woman?'" Accessed April 2, 2025. https://www.nps.gov/articles/sojourner-truth.htm.

Northrup, Solomon. *Twelve Years a Slave.* New York, 1853.

Ortiz, Paul. *An African American and Latinx History of the United States.* Beacon Press, 2018.

Peretti, Burton W. *Lift Every Voice: The History of African American Music.* Rowman & Littlefield, 2009.

Prahlad, Sw. Anand. *African-American Proverbs in Context.* University Press of Mississippi, 1996.

Shogan, Colleen. "'We Shall Overcome': Lyndon B. Johnson and the 1965 Voting Rights Act." White House Historical Association, April 8, 2021. https://www.whitehousehistory.org/we-shall-overcome-lbj-voting-rights.

Simama, Jabari. "Black Elected Officials and the Nuanced Issue of Expectations." *Governing*, March 29, 2022, https://www.governing.com/now/black-elected-officials-and-the-nuanced-issue-of-expectations.

Thibodeaux, Mary Roger. *A Black Nun Looks at Black Power.* Sheed & Ward, 1972.

United States Census Bureau. "Census Bureau Releases New Data on Minority-Owned, Veteran-Owned, and Women-Owned Businesses." US Census Bureau, October 26, 2023. https://www.census.gov/newsroom/press-releases/2023/annual-business-survey-employer-business-characteristics.html.

WGBH Educational Foundation. "John Brown's Holy War: The Hanging." Accessed April 2, 2025.

Wright, Richard. *Black Power: Three Books from Exile: Black Power; The Color Curtain; and White Man, Listen!* Harper Collins, 2008.

Zinn, Howard. *A People's History of the United States: 1492-Present.* Harper Perennial, 1980.

Image Sources

1 https://commons.wikimedia.org/wiki/File:Isom_Dart.jpg
2 https://commons.wikimedia.org/wiki/File:Slaveshipposter.jpg
3 https://commons.wikimedia.org/wiki/File:PowersBibleQuilt_1886.jpg
4 https://commons.wikimedia.org/wiki/File:Medgar_Evers_press_photo.jpg
5 https://commons.wikimedia.org/wiki/File:James_Forten_(cropped).jpg
6 https://commons.wikimedia.org/wiki/File:Elizabeth_Keckley,_1861.png
7 https://commons.wikimedia.org/wiki/File:Sojourner_Truth_with_Abraham_Lincoln.jpg
8 https://commons.wikimedia.org/wiki/File:Baker_Banana.jpg

www.ingramcontent.com/pod-product-compliance
Lightning Source LLC
Chambersburg PA
CBHW070339010526
44107CB00004B/555